DISCOVERING KINBAKU

What my Adventures in Japan Taught Me About the Art of Erotic Rope Bondage

ZETSU NAWA

D1304693

Copyright © 2019 Zetsu Nawa
All rights reserved.
ISBN: 9781099161933

DEDICATION

This work is dedicated to the memory of Yukimura Haruki, my teacher and mentor who showed me not only what rope could be, but how I could use it to open my heart to others. He left us far too soon.

TABLE OF CONTENTS

INTRODUCTION

This book is a collection of my writings from the past five years of studying kinbaku, both in the US and in Japan.

During that time, I have also been teaching rope in Los Angeles at my dojo. During that time I have taught close to 3000 students, with classes varying from 100 person demonstrations to hands on workshops and one on one private lessons.

Teaching rope is a way to pass on the things I have learned.

I have focused my writings, primarily, on trying to communicate what I have felt were the essential lessons I learned from Japanese bakushi, particularly aspects I felt were missing from the west.

I was incredibly fortunate to spend time with Yukimura Haruki, one of the legendary grandmasters of the art. As his student, I learned more that I can say about the power of rope to foster emotion, communication, and a shared experience that allows you to feel in ways that nothing else can match.

I learned the most from him not from his instruction in rope technique, but from the time we spent together before and after, often times talking for hours about rope, kinbaku, and the meaning of what we do.

When I first opened my dojo, I had a long conversation with Yukimura sensei about the responsibilities and obligations one incurs when you teach. He stressed the importance of understanding my students as people, not as customers, and to never lose sight of the challenges, difficulties, and potential heartbreak that rope can cause.

He also taught me the value of patience, freedom, expression, humor, and generosity. Things I try my best to model with my students. No matter how much I would struggle with a tie, concept, or pose, he was always there with a smile, a laugh, and a gentle correction to guide me.

The same has been true for most of the bakushi and models I have met in Japan. While I have learned how to tie, I have also learned something much more valuable: I have learned why tying matters, what it can be, and how I can share a part of myself in my rope, as well as get something in return.

There is nothing in these pages that will tell you how to do any particular tie or where to place the ropes or what knots to tie. What I want to communicate is what I see as the heart of shibari, its essence, its, to use a Japanese term, *kokoro*.

The best way, I felt, to do that is to show my own path, my own growth, my own *adventure* in rope, in the hope that others might be able to glean something of value from it.

It is a story of rope, but in particular, it is *my* story of rope.

This volume starts with a discussion with Yukimura sensei about the purpose of rope suspensions and it ends with a reflection on how we think about teaching and sharing rope today.

From that day in Ebisu to the present, my ideas about rope have shifted, grown, developed, and become more sophisticated as I have experience more and more in the world.

As I often tell my students, rope is about preference. But I also caution them that one cannot have preferences for things you have never seen, felt, or experienced.

By sharing my own experience, I want to help others understand what is possible with rope.

Nothing contained in these pages will help you tie, but it is my hope that at least something in these pages will help you reflect and will help you tie better.

Zetsu

YUKIMURA SENSEI ON SUSPENSION

October, 2014

At the end of our last lesson, Yukimura sensei was asked "Honestly, what do you think of suspensions?"

His response was a bit of a surprise.

Yukimura doesn't do many suspensions and is known for his floorwork and caressing style, far more than suspensions. So when he told us that eventually our lessons would include suspensions as part of Yukimura Ryuu, we were more than a little surprised.

He started off by explaining that when he was younger, he did a lot of them, but soon everyone was doing them and he wanted to be different. They were becoming a signature of Nureki and his feeling was that he should do something unique.

He went on to explain that suspensions put limitations on how you can connect with your partner. When you play on the floor, the range of communication, expression, and connection is unlimited and your play can range from soft and sensual to sadistic. Suspensions, he told us, are always "seme" (hard play).

Then he started to show us something amazing. He tied our model, Aya chan, into a kata ashi (single leg suspension) and talked about exposure, shame (hazukashii) and the various ways women will try to hide themselves while tied. There is a natural tendency, he explained, to bring the knees together and even though it is difficult and doesn't cover much, there is a kind of psychological comfort from trying.

And then he adds another rope and she is up, suspended in a full M-gi, legs open with nowhere to hide. Her reaction transforms immediately and we can see on her face, exactly what he is talking about. From struggling to full on shame—nowhere to hide.

Suspension, he explained, should emerge as a natural and organic part of what you are trying to accomplish and, in this case, it was a response from the model trying to hide herself and resist the exposure that made the suspension work.

The point for Yukimura is that there are some good reasons to do suspensions, but doing them just for the sake of doing them isn't enough.

LEARNING KINBAKU
EAST AND WEST

October 2014

While he was visiting Los Angeles, I had a very long discussion with Akira Naka about how he learned kinbaku.

I have been very lucky to spend time studying with some of the best Japanese rope artists, most recently hosting Naka Sensei here in Los Angeles. We spent a lot of time talking about how he learned from Nureki Sensei and the difference between learning in the traditional style in Japan and giving workshops in America.

I have also been accepted into the school of Yukimura Haruki, both as a student and as an instructor of his ryuu. Yukimura Sensei has given me a name, Haru Yutaka, and a license (menkyo) which authorizes me to teach his school of kinbaku. In have studied with him in the US when visited and many times in Tokyo while visiting him at his studio in Ebisu and at photoshoots in Roppongi.

I say this not to brag, but as a means to give some credentials to what I say about learning kinbaku in Japan. There are others with far more experience and training and who can probably say these things better than I can. But what I can offer is, I hope, more insightful than those who love to talk about it without experiencing it or who prefer glib dismissals to actually answering questions, I want to try to explain what makes learning rope in Japan different from learning rope in America.

The first thing you need to understand is that Japan and the US (and most of Europe) are radically different in one crucial aspect. The US is what Edward Hall, a cultural anthropologist, called a "low context culture" where Japan (and many Asian countries) are "high context cultures." That distinction is incredibly important to understand both the languages of these two cultures as well as how things are learned and taught. That difference determines how we think, what we hear, and how we process just about everything.

In low context cultures, such as the US, the clarity, precision, and accuracy of information is paramount. What is said is more important than who is saying it and the meaning is expected to be found in the things that are said.

As Brian Wilson summarizes it:

> People from low-context cultures value logic, facts, and directness. Solving a problem means lining up the facts and evaluating one after another. decisions are based on fact rather than intuition. Discussions end with actions and communicators are expected to be straightforward, concise, and efficient in telling what action is expected.

In a high context culture, like Japan, the priorities are reversed. Meaning is derived from the things surrounding the words, which are far more important than the words themselves and silence, as well as speaking, can be used as a very important tool for communication.

In Wilson's summary, he writes:

> According to hall, these cultures are collectivist, preferring group harmony and consensus to individual achievement. And people in these cultures are less gov-

erned by reason than by intuition or feelings. Words are not so important as context, which might include the speaker's tone of voice, facial expression, gestures, posture—and even the person's family history and status.

So how might this relate to teaching kinbaku? There are two ways, I think. First, by realizing that woven into the fabric of the art are the assumptions of a high context culture. The art itself does not translate well to the demands of a low context mindset. In fact, it can be enormously frustrating. One interesting thing I have witnessed on several occasions is a bakushi declaring "I never do" something only to witness them do that exact thing only minutes later. What they are saying is that "in this particular situation or at this time, I would never do a particular thing." However, when the situation changes, that thing may not only be acceptable, it may be required! Very confusing to the low-context mindset.

Which brings us to point number two. We frequently hear that knowledge in Japan is not "taught" but "stolen." Which is exactly what it looks like to a low-context mindset. It might be better explained as "knowledge isn't taught, so much as absorbed over a long period of time." When you consider a high context art in a high context culture, it begins to make sense.

To learn the art, you need to learn the context, because it is only in the context that the art has any meaning.

People in the West will look at kinbaku in Japan and conclude "there is no right way" because they aren't even consistent. They will say something in one place and something different in another and wrongfully conclude there is no discernible style, technique or school there.

Most schools of traditional kinbaku are teaching how to do the right thing at the right time in the right way. How do you know what that is? The answer that a high context person will give sounds like absolute bullshit to the low context mind. You just know. You know because the context tells you. You feel it.

My experience in taking classes with Yukimura Sensei is exactly like that. He will simply tell you to do something: Tie with one rope, with some feeling, Yukimura style. Then he watches and as a student you watch him. You know you are doing it well when he becomes engaged and starts to make "encouraging sounds" and occasionally will add an approving "Mmmmm hazukashii." Sometimes when I am really making a mess of things, he will stop me and correct what I am doing. No reason is given and the correction is quite gentle. All of the "meaning" of the correction is in the context. If Yukimura Sensei stops what you are doing and shows you something different, what you are doing is wrong. That will never be spoken, but it is felt. (Sadly, felt quite often by me).

From the perspective of low context, all the teaching happens on the tatami mat, watching and being instructed, being corrected and show approval or not.

From the high context perspective, learning happens over tea, over discussion, even at the moment you are greeted at the door. In every moment of interaction, you are "becoming a student" and the hands-on instruction is a small part and maybe the most insignificant part of that.

When Naka Sensei visited us in Los Angeles, I learned more about kinbaku from him in our hours of conversation than I did in any lesson or workshop I took, because I was learning the context of his kinbaku, the thing that gave it meaning.

It is also the reason I love to collect books. I am not looking for instruction or even inspiration from the books I read. I am immersing myself in a context of kinbaku, which finds its way into all the things I do.

During our workshops in LA, there were times when a student would ask Naka Sensei "why do you do that?" It could be as simple as a rope placement or the tying of a bow. Sometimes he would answer "because that is the way Nureki did it." To the low context learner, that is no answer at all. The few people I spoke to felt it meant "there is no real reason" or "it is just the way he was taught."

But for Naka those choices were part of what define the style. The "reasons" are so deeply embedded and so enmeshed in the nature of the art itself that it is impossible to separate them into something that can be easily explained. Naka's answer–because that is the way Nureki did it–was not saying there is no reason, it was giving you the only reason that mattered, the most important reason.

You can teach technique and you can "share knowledge" but in the end, kinbaku is something that cannot be taught; it must be felt. Right and wrong are terms that have radically different meanings and significance in high and low context cultures.

After studying with Yukimura Sensei, I would say "right" in Yukimura ryuu is in any given situation doing the things with rope that bring about the result that is in keeping with the basic tenets of Yukimura ryuu. "Wrong" is the feeling that in Yukimura ryuu you don't do that particular thing in that particular situation or that you can do it better some other way. Techniques are a toolbox you can draw on and the more you have, the "righter" you can be. Being a student of Yukimura means you are spending your time trying to figure out right from wrong, usually by tying.

The same seemed true for Naka Sensei. He would often talk of doing ties in ways that felt right, looked right, or made sense. He once told me his biggest confusion about western kinbaku was why some westerners would do things in ties that make no sense.

I told him "because that is how they were taught to do it." He nodded and gave a long and thoughtful "ahhhhh" and then I asked him if he understood what I meant and he said "no." It led to a very long discussion....

FOR BEAUTY AND EFFECT: TYING THE GOTE

November 2014

When I started learning kinbaku, the first tie I learned wasn't the takate kote. It wasn't the second or third of fourth tie I learned either. It wasn't until several months into my instruction that I learned a very basic gote. It was probably two years until I was shown a high hands tie.

Six years later, I am still learning about the gote. It is a tie of almost infinite complexity, possibility, and depth. It can be tied dozens, if not hundreds, of ways from one rope to three or four (or more).

The current debate raging in the west right now (and by that I mean the people sniping at each other on Fetlife) is whether or not the tie is "safe." What people mean by safe, as I understand it, is safe for suspensions, particularly dynamic ones.

My answer to that question is simple and direct. I have no idea. I have never done a dynamic suspension or a transition or any other type of kinbaku that would require me to consider that question. In the complex, diverse, and extensive world of kinbaku, dynamic suspensions are a tiny slice of what is the art has to offer.

What bothers me about the discussion is not the question of safety (I think we should always be asking ourselves about safety and how to improve it). What I dislike is the way the entire question has been reduced to an engineering problem.

The two reasons I tie a takate kote or gote have nothing to do with the safety of the engineering of it. The reasons I tie it are these: beauty and effect.

I find the takate kote, especially a high hands version, to be the most beautiful form of restraint I know how to do. It is simple in its elegance. It is an example, for me, of what might be considered shibusa (渋さ). It gives a strong feeling, one which encompasses simplicity without being simple. It is modest and natural, not showy or ostentatious. It has an element of imperfection. A beautiful gote is never neat or perfect. It is worn on the body and each body both shapes and is shaped by the tie. It is a tie of infinite complexity that appears on the surface to be simple and natural.

Even the most simple gote, such as the one we do in Yukimura ryuu (with one rope) can evoke in your partner some of the deepest feelings of surrender, helplessness, eroticism, shame, and desire. Its power is not just in the tie itself, but how it is tied. It is a tie that progresses gradually and creates layers upon layers of feelings and emotions. Once it begins your partner never loses the feeling of being tied and growing increasingly bound. The tie itself cannot be separated from the act of tying it.

No other tie I know allows me to combine these things, the beauty and power of a sense of aesthetics with the dramatic effect this tie can create.

Years ago, I was privileged to watch Nureki Chimuo tie a woman in Tokyo. As she was tied by him into a takate kote, she began to orgasm, not once, but multiple times. Nureki Sensei grew very cross with her and reprimanded her to stop it. "We have a very long day ahead of us and if you keep doing that, you aren't going to last," he told her. Nureki's style exemplified what I mean. Each gote he tied was like a masterpiece, but the way he tied made it all look so effortless.

When you watch a bakushi slowly draw his partners arms behind them, purposefully tie their wrists and wrap their arms around them, slowly drawing the rope across their skin, listening as their breathing changes, feeling the almost imperceptible shifts in their body. Their skin flushes and their eyes shut. Soft moans escape their lips as you secure the rope, feeling them fall back into you as you snap the last knot taut, pulling them off balance, helpless and exposed to you. You can feel, sense, hear, and smell everything happening around you. Your hearts beat in unison.

I step away and admire her, bound and posed just as I like her. She knows I am watching her but she can't quite bring herself to look into my eyes. Helpless and abandoned, even just for a moment. A beautiful object to be admired and inspected. She feels my absence now as strongly as she felt my presence before. There is a rawness to her beauty. Helplessly, she aches for my return.

That is my takate kote.

The person who then asks "Yeah but it this acceptably safe?" might just be missing the point.

THE CONNECTION AND THE IMAGE

November 2014

My introduction to kinbaku came in the form of an image on a computer screen 20 years ago. It was unlike anything I had ever seen before and set me on a journey that would bring me full circle. The image I would later learn was created by Sugiura Norio and this past Saturday, I found myself flying from Los Angeles to Tokyo to participate with a group of fellow photographers in Sugiura Sensei's "satsueikai" (photography group shoot).

Two years ago, I was introduced to many of the great bakushi in Tokyo, including Naka Akira, who would be doing the tying for the afternoon. Naka Sensei is truly inspirational in his rope work and the opportunity to photograph him up close just made the workshop that much more of a once-in-a-lifetime experience.

Within a few minutes of arriving, Sugiura Sensei had come in to greet us and was enthusiastically looking at my camera and going over the various settings with me, iso, shutter speed, white balance, discussing lighting and how the day would proceed. It was a surreal moment. Here I was sitting in Tokyo, speaking with Sugiura Norio and getting ready to shoot alongside him for the next 8 hours. I was so excited that I immediately sent a text back to my partner "OMG, Sugiura just helped me set up my camera!" to which she wisely responded, "Well you better pay attention and stop texting in class!" Of course, she was right, but I just had to share my enthusiasm. I was doubly delighted by Sugiura Sensei's excellent English, which made the whole day much easier than I anticipated.

I was also delighted to see Naka Sensei once again, who I had the pleasure of visiting with last time I was in Tokyo in July this year. He was, as always, full of good humor and very friendly and welcoming. His rope, as to be expected, was inspiring.

The shoot was held in an old-style Japanese house (as I understand it, it is owned by Naka Sensei) in Roppongi, which has the feel of many of the older Showa-style kinbaku photos I first admired, and was influenced by, in my appreciation of the art.

The model for the day, Shizuki Iroha (who I had also had the chance to meet and visit with last trip) was introduced and we set off to work. She posed briefly allowing for the first set of photos. Sugiura Sensei gave subtle and gentle guidance about position and how to hold her head as the sounds of shutters opening and closing filled the room. And then we were off.

For the first session, there were a dozen photographers, arranged in three groups with color-coded armbands. As each color was called, that group would be given preference for position and allowed to shoot for a few minutes until the next group was called. The second session after lunch was a smaller group of seven photographers.

Sugiura Sensei spent most of his time during the photo sessions directing assistants to move the lights to different positions and moving back and forth making small adjustments in Shizuki San's position. While Naka Sensei tied, they would discuss different ideas and possible arrangements. I could sense a strong partnership between bakushi and photographer as they worked together to create some beautiful opportunities for us to photograph.

Periodically, Sugiura Sensei would give me advice, "move there" or "get closer" or "shoot that!" During one photo set, I hear him call out my name. I stop shooting look up and he beckons me over. He points to a spot on the floor and motions for me to kneel down. I do and he nods enthusiastically. When I point the camera and look, I see the shot he is directing me toward and for a brief moment, I feel like I see the model through Sugiura Sensei's eyes.

As each tie progressed, Shizuki San seemed to feel the rope more deeply, on several occasions being moved to tears. The tears came not from the pain or endurance of difficult suspensions, but at times of quiet after the intensity of the tie had passed. It was very moving to watch, a personal expression of how deeply moved she had been by the experience of Naka Sensei's rope.

To photograph such a moment is always a struggle for me. On one hand, it is a moment of such beauty that capturing it is the essence of what I love about kinbaku photography. But it is also a moment so deeply personal and private, a moment where the model is so exposed and vulnerable that the obligation to capture and reflect it accurately is immense. For that photo to be worthy, it must be equal to the moment. A very high standard to meet!

This is what has always moved me about Sugiura Sensei's photography, his ability to capture and distill the essence of the moment–to capture the feeling. He is able to show on the outside what the model is feeling inside. And I watched carefully, trying to see how he does this.

I took careful note of how each set was lit. We shot with tungsten lighting, though when we spoke later, he confirmed when shooting solo he uses strobes. The combination of keeping the lighting tight on the subject and lighting from the sides and back, produce a feeling of both strength and solitude for the model and allowed for some dramatic shadowing in each set.

But the true moments of fascination for me were watching when something captured the attention and passion of Sugiura Sensei. He would quickly move to grab his camera and begin shouting instructions for lighting and to the model. His instructions grew more demanding as he shot, wanting more and more from her, pushing her harder and harder for the feelings and expressions he wanted to see.

In my study of rope in Los Angeles, we spend a lot of time talking about connection and communication through our tying and our rope. I have always thought of kinbaku photography as a way to capture that connection between bakushi and model and preserve it. Watching Sugiura Sensei shoot revealed to me how the photographer can create something that is also very special and very moving. There is emotion, connection, passion, and desire. But there is also a demand. When I asked Sugiura Sensei later what he was saying when he was instructing Shizuki San, he explained to me that he always wanted "more."

I did not understand the words, but the sentiment was clear: give me more of yourself, give me everything until there is nothing left. And time after time Shizuki San responded and did just that.

Even with more than a dozen people in the room, I could sense Sugiura Sensei's ability to create and foster an immediate and powerful connection, as he shot, pulling out from her exactly what he wanted and capturing it. We were all voyeurs in that moment, hoping to capture a part of what he was creating. There is a difference between creating that moment and witnessing it. And I could see Sugiura Sensei's passion creating the moment, the connection and communication with Shizuki San that would make that moment a special thing to capture.

As I looked at the pictures I took, I tried to focus on the ones which moved me the most, which ones created a feeling for me that reminded me of the connection and intimacy I felt during the day. I kept returning to the struggle I felt. Was I capturing what was so beautifully and elegantly revealed to me during that day? Was I being honest to the moment and truthful to my own feelings? It would not be enough to simply capture the beauty of Naka Sensei's rope or to simply record what had happened during the day. I would have hundreds of images that would do that.

All that remains is to express my deep thanks and gratitude to Sugiura Sensei, Naka Sensei and Shizuki San for an amazing day and experience and for how much I learned from each of you!

URAMADO: WEST MEETS EAST IN FETISH ART

January 2015

To those who study Japanese bondage, one of the most iconic and frequently mentioned magazines of the era is *Kitan Club*. As the earliest and most well known of the SM magazines it is regarded as one of the foundations of modern kinbaku and SM publishing.

Shortly after the *Kitan Club* began publishing SM content, another magazine appeared, which proved to be equally significant in the formation of Japanese kinbaku culture. That magazine was *Uramado* (translation "Rear Window"), which ran from 1956 to 1965 and billed itself as "The Japan's Most Remarkable S-M Magazine."

Launched by legendary author, artist, bakushi and publisher Suma Toshiyuki (known more commonly as Minomura Kou or by his artist name Kita Reiko) and later, in 1961, edited by Nureki Chimuo, *Uramado* was one of legendary publications of the time.

Suma Toshiyuki has been one of the early authors to play a significant role in bringing *Kitan Club* to prominence, especially the artwork he created under the name Kita Reiko. Moving to *Uramado* in 1956 marked a major shift in the SM publishing world.

More than any other magazine, *Uramado* featured western artists in its magazine, often running full "comics" or series in English. *Uramado* showcased many of Japan's best erotic artists, including Muku Youji and Harukawa Namio as well as the enigmatic Ishizuka Yoshiyuki. So it is not surprising that the magazine and its editors would have great interest in his American counterparts.

In 1961, *Uramado* created a section of the magazine title "海外の公刊誌より" (Published in Magazines Overseas) which featured art from a wide range of western artists.

In the 1950s and 1960s, exposure to Japanese erotic art was extremely limited in the West. While Japan was experiencing a massive explosion in SM publication, the west was much more limited in its sexual expression. The outlets for fetish, SM and bondage, were limited to a few mail order houses, most famously Irving Klaw's, and magazines such as John Willie's sporadic publication of *Bizarre*.

In *The Beauty of Kinbaku*, Master K documents the influence that Japanese rope art had on western artists, in particular John Willie, documenting a marked shift in his style that coincided with Willie receiving copies of Japanese bondage magazines from a correspondent in Okinawa, leading to Willie coping "a few ideas for use in his own photographs."

In the period from 1957-1961, Master K argues, Willie begins to "mimic classical kinbaku ties" and begins to incorporate classical Japanese elements such as bamboo poles and hashira, a classic element of Japanese architecture infrequently seen in the west.

While it is important to document the impact of Japanese rope on western tying practices, we must also understand that cross cultural communication flows in both directions. It is hard to imagine that images flowing into magazines as successful as

Uramado and to a lesser degree *Kitan Club* didn't shape and influence Japanese approaches to SM and bondage.

In spite of a wide range of expressions of BDSM found in western art, the work that appears in *Uramado* is almost exclusively female dominant. While most images focused on bondage show women restrained, themes of male submission are frequent as well. Almost entirely absent are images in which men take a dominant role, even as spectators.

Some of the earliest appearance of western fetish art in *Uramado* begin in 1962 (vol 6) under Nureki's editorship and feature the femdom art of Gene Bilbrew (using one of his many pseudonyms, VanRod).

In 1963, *Uramado* featured images from Ruiz, one of Irving Klaw's illustrators for his *Nutrix* series of publications. Ruiz work frequently featured female dominant/female submissive scenes and elaborate bondage.

Later in 1963 and in to the last full year of publication, *Uramado* featured the work of Eric Stanton, John Willie, and Jim of Switzerland, all of whom were established artists working with Klaw and distributed through his mail order services.

By the end of 1964, Uramado had published a number of photo shoots as well and several full length serials, published in English showing many of the west's finest fetish artists

門外不出

January 2015

Today I received a book in the mail that I have been searching for a long time. It is a book of paintings by Ozuma, one of the most well-known kinbaku and tattoo artists in Japan. He recently passed away and his books have been incredibly hard to find and astronomically expensive.

This book is a collection of his "Secret Art," mainly paintings of heavier women in rope, often times excessively so. The depictions are unusual because they are so different from Ozuma's normal art, though it should be said the women he painted were always larger bodied, especially by Japanese standards.

As I read more about the book, I learned it came out of a gallery show in 2009 where Ozuma had exhibited his 門外不出 or "Mongai fushutsu." Having no idea what those words meant, I spent a fair bit of time tracking down the meaning of the concept and I found it be something that made me reflect a bit, at least what limited understanding I was able to glean from what I read.

These were paintings Ozuma had done for years and years, but never published, exhibited or shown to others. They were his "secret art."

One definition of "Mongai fushutsu" I found is "seldom lending or showing something precious because one values it," something not shared with others, particularly outsiders. It is something kept secret not because it is shameful or dangerous. It is something kept private because it is precious.

It is neither greedy nor "elitist" nor is it particularly selfish. Things are not withheld out of malice or for control. They are withheld because their dignity demands it.

Sometimes to share a thing is to cheapen it.

It is a way of valuing something that we don't seem to have a feeling for in the west. Maybe the concept of something being "priceless" or having "sentimental value" comes close to it.

Our culture is one where sharing freely is considered one of the highest virtues. In a culture obsessed with the self, behaving selflessly has the appearance of moral rectitude.

Even when we do share things in the west, we attach an economic value to them. Anything can be had for a price. Anyone not willing to share all is labeled an "elitist" and shouted down. There is something inconceivable to us about the idea of someone dying with knowledge they never passed on being a beautiful thing.

It is very powerful to me to think about the inherent value of something being preserved by not sharing it, even by effacing its very existence.

While there are certainly those who delight in playing gatekeeper, even as they boast about never taking a dime for sharing what they know, make no mistake, they are taking their payment in ego gratification and narcissistic supply.

I can't help but think that maybe it takes a much stronger person to keep something precious close to their heart and not dangle it as bait or temptation to others. To not be the keeper of the sacred knowledge, but instead to be content and secure simply knowing what you know and what you have and just letting that be enough.

KINBAKU IN CONTEXT: READING NUREKI'S KINBIKEN

January 2015

When Akira Naka tells the story of how he learned rope, he begins with the story of Kinbiken, Nureki Chimuo's monthly rope salon in Tokyo that Naka san attended for five years. During that time, he watched, observed, and eventually assisted Nureki sensei with those events. It was close to two years before he was able to even touch rope and longer until he would actually tie himself.

In the West, such a story is often understood as a test of patience or a rite of passage. In Japan, it may be seen somewhat differently. The idea of building a context for rope is something we don't understand very well in the West and we teach even less. In part, because we don't have the same kind of patience and in part because we don't have the same resources to fill that context and understand things in the same way.

The value of Kinbiken was not simply in the transmission of technique nor in establishing a particular style of kinbaku. The value was in shaping a sense of what kinbaku could look like and, more important, feel like. Not only was Kinbiken a teaching environment, it was also a photo salon, the basis for videos, and the subject of multiple publications, books, and articles. Kinbiken itself was always more than just a monthly meeting, it was a context for kinbaku. The name itself is a shortening of the full description, Kinbakubi kenkyūkai, or "Beautiful Bondage Study Group."

Understanding Kinbiken can provide some greater insight into the history of rope in Japan, as well as provide some points of reflection for thinking about how we might interpret kinbaku in a western culture.

Recently, a discussion was started in Fetlife about the concept of kotobazeme, literally "word torture," in response to several of the interviews posted here. It occurred to me that it was a concept that was very difficult to understand from a non-contextual point of view. As I understand it, kotobazeme is essentially saying the right thing at the right time to help build the context of the scene. It will differ every time, based on the people involved and the energy and flow of the scene. It seems impossible to describe it as anything more than "using your words" to help create a scene or headspace.

Kotobazeme illustrates a feeling I have about Japanese rope. Kinbaku is never just about technique. Of course, technique matters for safety, for effect, for aesthetics, and so on. But the essence of kinbaku, for me, is not in any particular element of it, but in how those elements come together to create a shared moment. As a rope top, we are more than just riggers, we are curators of experience.

Knowing technique is like understanding the vocabulary of a language, but none of the grammar. You can use it to communicate in the most rudimentary ways, but to fully express yourself you need to know more than just words. You need to know how they come together and how they are related to other words, stories, and ideas.

A good rope scene has a grammar. Watching Nureki tie is

something of a masterclass in grammar. I had the privilege of doing it in person in 2011, for a photo shoot he did for Mania Club magazine. His technique comes across as effortless. The effect on his model, however, was intense. I understood watching that is was more than just the rope that was creating the scene.

There are many reasons to approach rope this way, but there are also reasons why we need to think seriously about the way we teach and think about rope in the West.

Perhaps the biggest risk, however, is for safety. More and more, I hear Western rope tops running into problems when they take a tie they have learned from a workshop and use it without giving thought to its context. We teach rope as if the content and context were separable.

When I read accident reports online, they often begin with a statement "We were doing an X-style suspension." Almost never do they start with "We were doing a rope scene." What is the difference and why does it matter?

I am lucky to own a few dozen videos of Nureki's Kinbiken workshops, many of the same ones that Naka likely attended as part of his learning rope. What is always interesting in Kinbiken sessions is how they start, how they build, and how they end. There is a gradual development. The scenes always start slowly, with basic ties, with long pauses for discussion and photography. Each segment is layered and built. The tie progresses, with each addition adding to the effect. The accumulation is not just of rope, but also emotion, psychology and physical response. There is beauty and elegance in such a progression, but there is also a measure of safety.

By the time the bottom is in a suspension, 20 or 30 minutes will have passed and a context will have been built. There is no sense of a "Nureki-style suspension." There is only a Nureki-style scene that ends in a suspension (usually but not always). The bottom is both becoming acclimated to the intensity but also their body is creating an almost euphoric feeling (not unlike a runner's high) which further protects them and allows them to go deeper into rope space.

It is easy to get bogged down in discussions of what something means or how to do a particular tie. The reality is that in an art as complicated and fluid as kinbaku, things mean different things at different times. Even more to the point, things mean *differently* at different times. Learning those differences and how to respond to them is not a matter of technique; it is a matter of experience, of feeling, and of empathy.

Understanding that nuance and the complexity of the context seems to me to be vital for understanding kinbaku at all. Spending time with Nureki's Kinbiken, and works like it, might help us begin to understand kinbaku as something more than technique.

ROPE AND CONNECTION: ICHI GO ICHI E

September 2015

Perhaps the biggest buzzword in rope today is "connection."

It is a difficult concept to put into words and even more so to teach. When people use the word connection, it is often a place-holder for a vague sentiment shared by rope partners that defies simple expression, a point of agreement that both people felt something, perhaps that the scene had powerful emotion, or that they experienced something beyond just sensation.

This is my effort to put into words what I mean when I talk about connection. It is my own personal reflection and for that reason alone probably idiosyncratic.

For me, connection has two components. One is the experience itself, the other is what I put into that experience and take away from it.

In Japan there is a saying "ichi go ichi e" (一期一会 "one time, one meeting") which has the sense of "once in a lifetime" or "never again" and it is often used to express the depth of meaning in valuing your time with other people. For me, connection in rope has that quality. When I am connecting through rope, it is with an awareness that the moment is for us, that is will never happen again, and that we are only together for the moment. That moment will reflect itself both into the past and color the future, as all events do, but this rope scene is our time together, never to be duplicated.

In that sense, every rope meeting is an opportunity. What we pour into that moment, for me, defines the concept of connection. When I think about my own personal sense of connection (and this, of course, can and should vary for everyone), the three things that have the most meaning to me are these: Honesty, Trust, and Vulnerability.

Honesty, at some level, requires a certain level of self-awareness. For me, connection begins with an honest expression not of what people want or do, but of who they are. Rope, like nothing else for me, can expose that. When I tie, I am opening myself up to an experience that reveals something very deep about who I am. It is about sexual fantasy, about desire, specifically about *my* desire. Bringing that honesty out of my partner is something I value as well. I want a partner who doesn't hide that or try to be something she is not. I value an honest expression in my rope and I try to offer an honest expression of myself through my rope. But that is just the starting point.

There must also be a level of trust between people. The sense that it is OK and safe to share that honesty. Honest expression without the fear of rejection is a cornerstone of connection. With trust, anything is possible. Without it, nothing is.

Which leads to the third, and most dangerous, element of connection: vulnerability. If there is honesty and trust, we are inevitably in a place of vulnerability. For me, as a bakushi, connection is about shedding expectations and a certain measure of certainty and security for the risks and rewards that come from making myself truly vulnerable to another.

It is easy to think of the bottom as the vulnerable person. They are, after all, tied up and helpless. But that is only a small part of the vulnerability to which I am referring. Vulnerability is less a physical state than a psychological one. At my best, when I tie, I hope my partner can truly feel me: my passion, my desire, my fantasy.

They are getting a glimpse at my psyche without filters, without restriction, and without the everyday noise that prevents people from truly communicating with one another.

For there to be connection, that vulnerability must be reciprocal. I want to experience my partner unfiltered. In some cases, rope allows me to do that. There is no guarantee that I can elicit that. In that sense, the possibility for connection starts with the bakushi's vulnerability. Without it, there can be no reciprocation.

My recipe for connection is simple:

When I tie for connection, I am at my most open, most honest, most truthful, and most vulnerable. For that one time. For that one moment For that one meeting.

Ichi go ichi e.

PLAYING WITH SHAME: THE ART OF SHUUCHINAWA

December 2015

In kinbaku there are many approaches and philosophies that animate our tying. Where techniques like *semenawa* are designed to stress the body and create an intense experience of physical endurance, as lesser known approach called *shuuchinawa* is designed to provoke a more psychological response based on shame and exposure.

One of the aspects of *shuuchinawa* that makes it difficult for many people in the west to understand is grounded in the relationship between sex and culture. In the west, specifically in the US, sex is strongly connected to and, in a way, regulated by our religious history and foundations. Western culture, through Christianity, has had a longstanding conflict with sexuality, especially the way we connect guilt and pleasure. Like most things we regard as pleasurable, sex is seen as sinful and, as a result, manifests certain feelings of guilt when it is exposed publicly.

In Japan, there is a limited or even non-existent connection between sex and guilt. And this is why *shuuichinawa* is much more grounded in a sense of shame, rather than guilt. That is to say, in Japanese culture there is no sense of religious guilt, no sense that sex is wrong or bad or that pleasure is in some sense sinful.

The taboo is Japan is much more animated by the division between the public and the private. The line between the two is extremely important in Japan and the idea of exposing something meant to be private in a public way is more a matter of appropriateness than right or wrong. It is embarrassing and shameful to call attention to yourself at all, much less in a way that is about something as private and personal as your sexuality.

The essence of *shuuchinawa* comes not from the guilt of sexuality, but from the shamefulness of being seen. There is nothing wrong with enjoying sex in Japan, but there is something inherently shameful about others seeing such a private and personal expression.

The shamefulness is amplified by the distance that is created by social status.

What often appears to be cosplay to the western audience (dressing as nurses, secretaries, stewardesses) is actually an exercise in taking positions of social status and using them to emphasize the contrast between the public face of the model and her private expressions of desire.

A costume can be much more than just a visual cue or stimulus. It is also a reminder of distance between a women's social status and face and her personal sense of her sexual desire. In short, it is the exposure of the desire, rather than the desire itself that creates the feeling of shame.

The connection between rope, shame, and humiliation in the west often focuses on creating a feeling of helplessness and making the bottom do the things they really want to do, but are in some way prohibited from feeling or doing by cultural or social mores. It is a *liberation* of desire.

In Japan, the dynamic is quite different. By binding and exposing a woman, it is an act of exposing her desire and making something private public. The shame comes from the tension between the sexuality of the private and the propriety of the public. It is an *exposure* of desire.

The greater the distance between the two, the more intense the feelings of shame and exposure.

Special thanks to Yukimura sensei, Nuit de Tokyo and Ugo for a very useful discussion of this topic in Ebisu.

CHIBA EIZO AND THE ART OF FACE TORTURE: THE PSYCHOLOGY OF SHAME

December 2015

During my recent visit to Japan, I had the privilege of meeting with one of the great bakushi in Japan who is less well known in the west. Chiba Eizo has been involved in kinbaku and humiliation play for most of his adult life and his history goes back to the beginnings of contemporary kinbaku culture in Japan.

Best known for his humiliation videos featuring nose and face play, he got his start as a bakushi very early on. Chiba san is part of the second generation of kinbaku practitioners who were influenced by the early works and writings of the WWII generation in Japan.

His interest, like many of his generation, began early, roughly at the age of 10, when he first encountered bondage and SM magazines such as *Kitan Club* and *Uramado*. The feelings for and love of SM goes beyond those early influences, he told me, "I think, maybe, before I was born, I was Marquis de Sade."

Chiba san is best known for his love of face bondage and nose play. For the last 20 years, he has run a small study group called Tanbikai, which translates to Aesthetic Society, to explore this unique and specifically Japanese fetish.

Much to my surprise, Chiba san explained that he didn't start out liking or even understanding nose play. After seeing nose hooks used for the first time, he said "I could understand why they do that. She's beautiful. Her face is beautiful. Why did he destroy her face? I couldn't understand nose torture."

After years of doing kinbaku, he began to look at things differently. When he was 30 or 35, he recalls, he began to ask a different question: "Suddenly I felt that 'Yes, they destroyed the beauty of her face, but now I am interested in inside her brain. What was happening in her brain when they tortured her nose?'"

The shift marked a fundamental change in how Chiba san began thinking about kinbaku as well, that perhaps there was another level beyond just binding her body. "Watch her eyes," he said, "maybe she felt sad. Maybe she felt ashamed." In her eyes, he saw not only resistance and refusal, but also a feeling, "like she was dreaming something." He began trying to understand what that refusal and resistance represented. "Maybe," he thought, "this is the final restraint of her mind."

As Chiba san described the process, the psychological dynamic became the center of our discussion. There is something particularly Japanese about nose torture because, as a culture, the concept of "face" is a central part of the cultural psyche. As he explained it, "the nose is the center of the face. The nose is the center of human pride." When a man or a woman endures nose torture, you are dealing immediately with their sense of self and their sense of pride.

But it is also a form of play that cuts right to the heart of the

SM dynamic. While professionally Chiba san often works with models for videos and productions, his true pleasure comes from playing with masochists or "true M-jo" in the vernacular of Japanese SM.

For Chiba san, this is the heart of the SM dynamic and fundamentally altered how he thought about humiliation play. While he initially thought of nose torture as deformation or destruction, as he came to better understand the psychology of this sort of play, viewing its function as a means of power exchange as well. As he explained, "Now, I don't say destroyed, but something different. Maybe she thinks, 'I have to obey him perfectly because the center of her pride is called by him.'"

It was that sense of connection or *kankei* that he wanted to explore in his SM play The essence of SM, as he describes it, is a blend of heart (kokoro), connection (kankei), and communication and it always begins with rope.

"Bondage, shibari, is very important when starting SM. She likes me or she hates me, according to how I use rope. So the rope starts the communication between myself and the M-jo. If she refused my rope, she could not go further (to nose play). And finally, I do this, nose torture or face torture."

What he would go on to describe is the manner in which he creates a psychological connection with his bottom. The process always begins with refusal and the goal is to move to acceptance of, even desire for, the surrender of one's pride and self to another. This is what Chiba san describes as *kankei*, a word for connection or relationship with the overtone of sexuality.

"When she accepts face torture, the distance between she and I is extremely close. So I think face torture and nose torture is very important. That is what I mean by the final restraint."

What makes this fundamentally different than other forms of play (including other humiliation play such as enemas) is the relationship between mind and body. I asked Chiba san how nose play differs from traditional forms of kinbaku. The element of shame and pride, which is central to how he sees this form of torture, makes the connection different, "Yes she is called by rope," he explained, "She isn't free. She can't move her body. But she still has her pride."

Perhaps the most interesting point of our discussion came when he explained the core dynamic of refusal. Nose torture, in the most basic sense, is a form of seduction. The challenge is not just to cause shame or humiliation, but to move past it, to a state of acceptance and even pleasure. When that is achieved, Chiba san says "I can see her heart, I can see what is happening inside her heart."

In one case, he described a woman who came to him from Europe, wanting to experience nose torture. As he described the scene, she didn't refuse and as a result he felt she also "didn't accept with a full heart."

Acceptance is more than just allowing the nose torture to take place or enjoying the sensation or humiliation. It is the transformation of the bottom's mind and psyche that is important.

"But when her pride is called by me, the nose is some sexual tool. First, they refuse. Second, they refuse. Third they refuse. But the fifth or the tenth, she accepts the nose torture and eventually she is even pleased by nose torture."

The goal for Chiba san, as he describes it is to get the M-jo to "accept with a full heart" and in order for that to happen, the meeting must begin with a refusal, with resistance, because it is in the overcoming of pride that he finds true acceptance in her heart. Seeing her this way, creates the transformation. "This makes a second face for her. Her other face. But not only another face, another mind."

The description of that "other face" and that "other mind" are linked for Chiba san. The goal and purpose of this kind of play is to move past the refusal and the shame and humiliation to the point where, as he would say, "the center of her pride" is called by another and the distance between the two is removed. At that moment, the moment of acceptance, nose torture becomes a uniquely sexual pleasure, where one's complete surrender of pride becomes the ultimate act of submission and also an ultimate act of connection between two people exploring the essence of *kankei*.

While I must admit to a long-standing fascination with nose play and face torture myself, spending the day with Chiba san and having the opportunity to delve into his decades of experience and his own personal reflections has done a lot to deepen my own understanding of this form of play and to remind me of the complexity and beauty of SM play.

On a personal note, it was a conversation that transformed my thinking about a lot of different aspects of SM, kinbaku, and fetish play. It was a reminder that no matter how we express our desires, the essence of kinbaku for me always comes back to *kokoro* and *kankei*, heart and connection.

My deepest gratitude to Chiba san for making it a very special day to remember and for giving me much to think about on my own journey in rope and SM play.

A special thank you to Damon Pierce and Digital Dark for helping arrange my meeting with Chiba san.

THE HEART OF KINBAKU

December 2015

At the beginning of December, I visited Japan. It was a trip that was a personal journey for me for a lot of different reasons, not the least of which was an effort to try to answer a question that has been running around in my head for a very long time: *What is the heart of kinbaku?*

The word frequently used in Japan for heart is *kokoro*. It means heart, the same way it does in English, with the nuance of spirit, strength, essence. Just as we might say someone has a lot of heart or we are getting to the heart of the matter, in Japan you might use *kokoro* to express a similar feeling.

The question was important to me for many reasons, not the least of which is my own desire to explore kinbaku at a level that fulfills me at a deeper level. So asking this question: "What is the heart of kinbaku?" was something I was hoping to answer for myself but also something I was hoping I could share in my teaching and workshops with students.

When I got to Japan, I asked a number of people the question and I was answered with the kind of responses that makes one think I was not being completely understood.

Either I had asked one of those questions that is so deep and profound that answering it is impossible (such as "what is the meaning of life?") or I was asking a question that didn't make a lot of sense to the people who were trying to answer it. I hoped it was the former, but suspected it was the latter.

The responses varied across the board, but they were all fundamentally unsatisfying.

Until I came to a stark realization a few weeks later. What if I was asking the wrong question?

As I began to reflect on the answers I got, I came to realize that perhaps I had framed the question in the wrong terms.

Asking a bakushi "what is the heart of kinbaku?" is like asking an artist, "what is the heart of a paintbrush?" Kinbaku itself has no "heart" to speak of, but is only an instrument for the expression of the hearts of those who tie and are tied.

With that shift in perspective, the answers I received became much clearer. If kinbaku is a tool for the expression of one's own heart and a means to find and open the heart of another then asking about its heart doesn't make very much sense.

There is something uniquely human about shibari and kinbaku. For me, that is emotional connection, that is heart. Every heart is, of course, different and every tie is a different expression of one's heart.

Kokoro is not, and can never be, in the rope or in the tie or in the technique. *Kokoro* is in the people who are engaging, communicating, and sharing themselves with each other, not the rope or technique.

In the West, it seems, that we all too often spend our time giving classes, workshops, and lectures on the tools, with not enough understanding of why we are using them.

While a paintbrush is an essential ingredient in creating a great work of art, it is no more than the vessel or tool that the artist uses to communicate something inside him or herself and share it with others.

Perhaps the most important lesson from this trip to Japan for me was that the heart of kinbaku doesn't reside in rope, our teachers, or Japan. It resides in each and every one of us. It was with me all along. It took a trip to Japan, 5000 miles away, to finally understand that my *kokoro* is always with me, no matter where I go. The hard part, the journey, is discovering it in yourself and learning to use your rope, your ties, and your skills to share it with another.

HAIKU OF ROPE

January 2016

I have been thinking a lot about the relationship between rope and words, particularly in relation to the practice of tying.

I was struck by a memory of a trip to Tokyo in 2011, where I came across a small statue garden. It was a tribute to Matsuo Bashō, the 17th century haiku master. It was no more than a half a dozen small statues coupled with haiku. It was inexplicably moving to just sit in this space and feel the weight of 400 years of history, meaning, and emotion surround me. Since that encounter, I have been curious about that form of poetry.

We all learn about haiku at some point. It is a form of poetry that follows a basic structure. Three lines. 5 syllables, 7 syllables, 5 syllables.

For most people, our first encounter with haiku is a matter of fitting words into the pattern. Making the haiku is the goal. It becomes a fun kind of game to fit one's thoughts into the pattern. The constraints and rules become a structure that defines the activity. Haiku is, in that sense, three lines, 5-7-5.

For most people fitting the words to the pattern is all haiku will ever be. There is a lot one can do in that space. Words are a near infinite resource and playing with them in the patterns of haiku can provide an endless supply of fun, experimentation, and opportunities for creativity.

Rope can be the same. It where we all start, because it is the only place we can start.

This is the essence of form.

It doesn't help answer the question that initially inspired me. What makes the poetry of Bashō survive for 400 years?

So one starts to dig and ask the question, why? Why that structure? Why did he use those words?

A world starts to open up. You begin to learn about *kireji*, the "cutting word," that gives structure to the form and divides the haiku, creating a juxtaposition of two parts of the verse. How the cutting creates emotion.

When the cutting word is placed at the beginning, it invites a comparison. When placed at the end, it creates a circular structure, inviting the reader back to the beginning to read again, now with a new perspective.

For example, a haiku writer may use や ya as a cutting word in the first line, dividing the haiku into two parts or 哉 kana at the end of the verse to express strong emotion and invite reflection. These become the conceptual elements of haiku, where language becomes more poetry. The use of *kigo* or seasonal words function as metaphors to evoke feelings of the seasons and nature, the traditional subject of haiku.

Rope can be the same. As we delve deeper into the art of kinbaku, we understand the purpose of the patterns and the forms, and we begin to tie differently. We are no longer simply obeying the form or pattern, we are now using it to create meaning. We start to tie conceptually, rather than technically. Timing, tension, touch, and breathing (and other things a well) become our *kireji*. The create our emotion, they divide our ties, they communicate more than just rope or pattern.

At the highest level, haiku transcends all of the constraints of the form, even while embodying it. Just as the seasonal nature of haiku is never just about the seasons, at our very best, our rope is never just about the rope.

Words, like rope, have the power to convey so much more. What make both beautiful is their ability to touch our heart, our essence. In Japanese, the word is *kokoro*.

The haiku of Bashō survives and is celebrated because it has the ability to touch each of us in a way that is unique to every individual, yet able to exist within the constraints of the form. It is the ability to *transcend* the form by fully and completely embracing and embodying it that elevates his work to something more than just haiku.

In the case of Bashō, he was famous for taking traditional subjects of haiku and giving them a new inflection which would both embrace the old, while also creating something fresh and new. The beauty and play of the haiku is the emergence of something playful resulting from the application of constraint to the imagination. To evoke, for example, an image from a sound.

So too it is with our rope. How do we evoke an emotion, a feeling, a connection, with something as physical as a length of rope?

Perhaps Bashō's most famous haiku can say better in 17 syllables what I have tried to communicate so far:

古池や蛙飛びこむ水の音
an ancient pond / a frog jumps in / the splash of water
Bashō, 1686

TYING THE ONE
ROPE GOTE

May 2016

When I think about tying, I think about the one rope gote. It is one of the easiest ties to do, but one of the most difficult to master.

I first learned the one rope gote from Yukimura sensei in 2011. It was unlike anything I had ever learned to tie. It had a simple but very unique construction. Tie the wrists, wrap twice around the chest, catch the ropes and create the nawajiri, the point of connection, control and communication.

Learning the technique itself takes an hour, maybe less if you are a more adept bakushi than I am.

Every time I would come back to see sensei and tie it, I would learn something new. Not new technique, but something different–a choice, a consideration, a feeling. The little things became big things. Things I had been doing without thinking became important to think about.

Over the next five years I came to realize two things. First, the point of the gote was not to make my partner feel the rope, it was to make her feel me through the rope. This is harder to do than it sounds. During my last visit, sensei would ask the model, "Could you feel him through the rope?" and he would be very stern with her and tell her "don't lie. It is important to know the truth." It was the most important question. Really it was the only question.

The second lesson I learned from Yukimura sensei is that the more you tie in his style, the less you know. It took me five years to understand and accept that. Every gote I tie is different and every time I share myself through my rope, I am different. Technique can get in the way of that realization. It can block you from sharing what is in your heart. The risk is that you become the pattern, the design, the tie itself, rather than the tie being an expression of you. If your rope doesn't start with heart, with feeling, it will never be anything more than just technique.

Mastering the gote, even a simple one rope gote, is partly mastering yourself and learning to make the rope an extension of yourself. It is your tool for communication. It is your means of expression. Like words it is multifarious, layered, complicated, filled with nuance and meaning. Technique is merely grammar and vocabulary. You need it to communicate, but alone it isn't going to allow you to say very much.

It is the difference between reciting someone else's poem and writing your own.

I like to think of my rope as a conversation where rope, reactions, and intentions take the place of words. It is something I do with my partner, not to them.

So how do I get my partner to feel me through my rope? That is a much harder question to answer. I can teach you the technique in an hour. I am not sure the rest can be taught. But it can be learned. That learning is a process which requires mindfulness, reflection, attention, and presence.

Over the years there are many things Yukimura sensei has said to me that made a deep impression. Almost all of them were things I thought I understood at the time. Almost all of them have produced moments of clarity or revelation at a later time. Those are the "Ah ha!" moments where I finally got what it was that he meant, sometimes months or even years later. They are deceptively simple ideas that become complicated and nuanced with experience.

Sometimes Yukimura would say things like "the first attack of the gote is the essence of Yukimura Ryuu." In one sense that tells you everything, but in practical terms it tells you nothing. What it told me was to pay attention to that moment and see what I could learn about how I communicate with my partner and how she communicates back to me.

After 100 gotes, I knew more. After 1000, even more. Finally, there is no technique and no knowing, there is only feeling and if your mind is mired in technique you will miss the moment altogether.

I know the next gote will be different, the feeling will be different, the moment will be different, the reaction will be different. In that moment, I have to realize I know nothing and trust that feeling is everything.

It all happens in the blink of an eye, the moment where rope touches skin, where the first pressure is applied, where your touch transmits your intention, your emotion, your mental state.

To make matters worse, almost all of the magic is invisible. When we starting thinking past technique, we integrate our feeling and emotion into our actions. They disappear into the rope. There are no wild gestures, flinging of rope, or dramatic moments.

There are dozens of things that sensei shared, some of which

I understand and some of which I hope will become more clear with time. Technique is static, it changes very little over time. At its best, it gets distilled to its essence, it becomes safer or more effective. Heart is the opposite–ever evolving, ever changing, it is the dynamic essence of how I see rope and how I want to tie.

What Yukimura sensei left behind was not technique, but a philosophy. It is a way of thinking about rope that opens a door to a lifetime of learning and growth. I do not think I will ever exhaust the resources he gave me.

The technique takes an hour to learn. The rest requires a lifetime.

AIBUNAWA AND SEMENAWA: PLEASURE AND ENDURANCE

June 2016

Not long before Yukimura sensei passed away I was lucky to be able to spend some time with him in Ebisu. A big part of our lessons always involved discussion. In fact on one particular day, our discussion went on for hours after the lesson was over.

Eventually, our conversation turned to a discussion of *aibunawa*, Yukimura's caressing style, and *semenawa*, a more intense and often painful form of rope play. Much to my surprise, Yukimura mentioned that in his earlier days his style was much harder and much more in the tradition of *seme*.

In the West, *semenawa* has been translated as "torture rope" and has a heavy emphasis on pain. Those who enjoy intense pain play will often describe their rope as *semenawa*. *Semenawa* however is not quite that simple. It is not just about hurting your partner or even causing pain.

It is a term that Yukimura used with a great degree of subtly and nuance. In his thinking, *seme* is never *just* pain or pain for pain's sake. It is suffering and endurance for a purpose and as much a mental state as a physical one. The question we need ask as a top is not just "what is she feeling?" but also "In what state is her mind when she feels it?"

The example Yukimura used was based on a simple tie: wrists tied together and raised over the head.

He began his demonstration by teasing the model once her wrists were tied. He tells her he is going to touch her tits and she blushes and turns away, her bound wrists clenched to her body. He passes the rope through a point over her head and raises her wrists, slowly and gently, slowly pulling her juban away from her body, beginning to expose her.

Once her elbows are above her breasts, just about shoulder height, he secures the rope and begins to play with her clothing, exposing her more. This, Yukimura explains, is *aibunawa* or "caressing rope." For the model, she has the feeling she can *almost* protect herself. She has the illusion that she has some control, but slowly finds she does not. The tie (and the person tying her) are too clever and have placed her ability to demure *just out of reach*. It becomes a game, an interaction between top and bottom, involving give and take.

Yukimura would frequently talk about tying loosely, to create the illusion that escape is possible. However, once the model tries, she finds the rope holds her. But it is the freedom to explore and to move, to walk the line between freedom and restraint, that animates the session.

The essence of this style is pleasure. It is, in Yukimura's words, releasing a woman's eros and playing with it.

For the second part of the demonstration, Yukimura re-positions the rope, pulling it taut and stretching the model's hands over her head, extending her completely. In this position, she is bound tight and unable to even struggle.

"This," Yukimura explains, "is semenawa."

The reason why has nothing to do with pain. Yukimura explains that it is not the rope that is controlling the scene, it is the creation of a particular headspace. She is exposed and helpless and there is nothing she can do. No illusion and no sense that maybe she can move or protect herself. Her body is stressed and stretched by the rope. She has no choice but to endure, which, he explains, is the essence of *semenawa*. Now when he touches her the emotion, response, and feeling is different. She has no choice. There is no play and there can be no resistance. Now she accepts the touching with a sense of surrender. It is something she has no choice but to endure.

The use of physical pain can be one conduit to make your partner feel that sense of endurance, but it is not the only one. Discomfort, emotional or psychological intensity, predicaments achieved through stressing the body or positioning all can create the feeling of something that needs to be endured.

One of the exercises Yukimura sensei did with me was to go through a number of different ties to show how each could be tied in a caressing style and in a seme style. The difference in each case had to do with the type of play in which the top would engage and the headspace it would create for the bottom. The ties themselves varied only slightly in their construction or application, but the effect of each was dramatically different. Even Yukimura's one rope gote, the foundation of many *aibunawa* ties, can be transformed into *semenawa* with just a single small adjustment.

Semenawa need not be painful (though it certainly can be and often is). It is more important that is creates a feeling of endurance and helplessness within the rope.

Aibunawa and *semenawa* are different methods of rope and, but more important, they are different ways of communicating your emotion, your intention, and your feeling to your partner.

ROPE AND KINDNESS

August 2016

Sometimes the impetus for reflection comes from the most unlikely places. A few years ago, I bought a woodblock print by Toshikata titled "Yamanouchi Kazutoyo's Wife." It tells the story of Chiyo, a young samurai's wife, who uses money she has saved to buy him the best horse she could find, a symbol of status and stature that would fuel his rise to power in the Sengoku period. When I saw the print, it reminded me in a very personal way a profound act of kindness that someone had done for me and I knew I had to own the print. Upon seeing it, I was moved and learning the story I was brought back to that memory in a very visceral way.

Recently, I have been thinking a lot about what is missing in the rope community as I see it. There is and always has been plenty to critique in the rope world and in the world of BDSM more generally. But what I see lacking the most is kindness.

That may seem an odd thing to look for in the midst of people tying each other up and often doing things that we call torture or torment. But in the immortal words of Nick Lowe, sometimes you need to be cruel to be kind.

As I see it, kindness is nothing more than the quality of seeing another in a profound and real way and taking an action that is neither necessary nor requested, in order to recognize them. It may be as small as a kind word or as dramatic as buying them a horse (OK, admittedly an outdated gesture). But the essence of kindness is taking the time to see who a person is and what a person needs, perhaps even when they can't see it themselves, and giving them something special and deliberate in a way which enriches both people's lives. That has always been the goal I strive for when I tie.

The root of kindness is never ego. Nor is it transactional. It is not about what you can get from another. It is about what you can give, without expectation or requirement of reciprocity. It is a giving, rather than a taking.

But kindness is not sacrifice. It is not something given at one's expense, but rather it is fulfilling because it is what we can be when we are at our most human. It makes us vulnerable to be kind. Perhaps that is why it happens less often than it should. It is actually quite hard to understand why an act which enriches those who both give it and who receive it happens with such relative infrequency. In a world (and a community) where harsh criticism, argument, envy, greed, jealousy, and competition are so prevalent, why is kindness so scarce?

Perhaps, because we, as a culture, are quick to mistake kindness for weakness or a lack of dominance. We fear being taken advantage of or seen as foolish. Nothing could be farther from the truth. Kindness takes strength. It takes wisdom. It takes insight. Occasionally it even may mean treating people better than they deserve.

So what does it mean to be kind with our rope? I believe it means taking the time to understand our partner, our connection, and our selves. It means that rope can and should be an act of giving, rather than taking. It also means seeing the best in what others do, assuming they mean well. Perhaps if we treated others with kindness rather than scorn, they might rise to the occasion and meet our expectations of them.

The language of consent has become dominated by the discourse of transaction, about what we are permitted to take, the limits on our behavior. We even call them "negotiations" which presumes the two sides want different things and we can reach some agreement on how each side can make the best deal to reflect their interests.

While I am not suggesting we no longer negotiate, what I do suggest is that perhaps there is a way of thinking about a rope scene less as a question of "what do I want?" and more of a question of "who is my partner and what do they need?" Then tending to those needs with a logic of kindness. In think in doing so, we are much less likely to violate boundaries or consent.

There is, in the end, no downside to adding acts of kindness, both small and large, to our scenes and to our community.

As Aesop wrote, "The level of our success is limited only by our imagination and no act of kindness, however small, is ever wasted."

ROPE: COMMUNITY AND CULTURE

December 2016

During my recent trip to Japan, I was struck by a recurring theme. In four separate conversations with some of the older rope artists in Japan, each spoke of how difficult it was when they first started out to find partners to tie. When Chiba Eizo started tying, he told me, it was almost impossible to bring the topic up with your partner as it was considered to be "extremely perverted." For decades even professional bakushi had difficulty finding models to tie.

One person even speculated that one of the reasons Nureki and Akechi got so good at rope was that they had access to more bottoms than anyone else. They got to practice all the time, so they were able to improve quickly in their technique. Finding women to tie was extremely challenging and kinbaku was something that was very much "underground" and the desires attached to were considered "abnormal" by most.

If you look back to the time when rope was becoming more visible in Japan, after the war, it is a time marked by a lot of turmoil and social conflict. Not unlike the US, Japan was wrestling with concepts of public morality and decency. In the 1950s, there were obscenity trials related to SM, including having one of the most famous SM magazines, *Kitan Club*, shut down for most of 1955 after their April issue was seized by the government.

During the "White Cover Period" (白表紙時代) of *Kitan Club*, which SMPedia defines as 1955 – 1967, the magazine only had 4 main models. While other models show up in smaller roles or as subjects of photos for sale, only four women are consistently active as models over this 12-year period. For more than a decade, *the most famous rope magazine in Japan featured only four main models*, and if you include others, the grand total of women in *Kitan Club* for that time period only expands to about three dozen.

This is also the period where may of the first generation of Japanese bakushi were growing up and first becoming exposed to rope bondage. Most of them, when asked, would also point to those magazines as a primary reference for learning how to tie.

The result of this activity being both underground and difficult to engage in has resulted in, what I believe, is a *culture of rope*. I mean that in the broadest sense. There is a significant history that has led to a shared set of values and beliefs around kinbaku in Japan that operates tacitly. A lot of that was probably absorbed through the stories and content that filled the magazines of the day as well.

Having a rope culture means that there is a complex context for rope that is well and deeply understood by those who practice it, usually learned through participation and observation over a long period of time. Cultural understandings are things you know but may not be able to articulate. They guide your actions and perceptions, without ever being made explicit.

Kinbaku as a Culture of Appreciation

The rope culture of Japan, I believe, is rooted in and still reflects the history from which it emerged. It is a culture that I would describe as one of appreciation. By that I mean that there is a certain amount of respect afforded not only to those who practice rope, either a tops or bottoms, but an appreciation for the *opportunity to engage in kinbaku at all.* To this day, it colors how many see rope and how they manage their relationships with other rope tops and, more importantly, with their rope bottoms.

The point I want to make is that because of its long tradition and history, kinbaku in Japan has developed a sense of culture, which is fundamental to understanding it as a practice.

In Japan (or at least in Tokyo, which is the only kinbaku in Japan I have any sense of) there is also a rope community. The community, or more properly communities, because they are always multiple, is where differences in practice, philosophies, and values get worked out. Not everyone likes each other. There are clubs, events, meetings, rope salons, and classes. But all of these things operate in the broader culture of rope in Japan, which is a shared understanding and context of what kinbaku is and how it fits into the larger world.

If we contrast this to the US and Europe, there is a significant difference.

In the West, kinbaku is a relatively recent phenomenon. Arguably, it hasn't really been a significant part of the western SM world until the past decade or so. There hasn't been much time to develop a culture of rope and what has passed as rope culture has usually been borrowed from Japan.

When we have been able to develop in the west is a sense of community. That community has really grown and blossomed in the past few years. For a decade, there was only a single rope conference in the US and only a slightly longer history of kinbaku in Europe. But recently, rope events have exploded in number, each expanding our sense of community. The number of classes alone in most areas has made kinbaku accessible in a way it has been before, even in Japan. Our communities are based on these shared experiences and practices.

Kinbaku East and West

The difference between Japan and the west, is that technique in the west was able to develop practically overnight. Our communities developed almost exclusively as communities of learning and practice, without an underlying culture of appreciation. Compared to Japan where you were mostly likely learning from magazines and lucky if you could ever find a partner willing to even be tied, the west has an overabundance of learning opportunities without the stigma of perversion that made finding bottoms next to impossible.

I believe there is a culture of kinbaku in west that is developing, but the way it is taking shape is fundamentally different from what happened in Japan.

Because in the west, we have never faced shortages of partners, struggles of censorship and indecency, or the need to develop technique, we haven't seen our culture develop in the same way. We have had our kinbaku technique handed to us after 50 or 60 years of development and as a result the skills that took decades to develop in Japan are now being transmitted in weekend workshops.

The level of skill in the west is on par with Japan, even according to many of the top Japanese bakushi, and that happened almost overnight.

The flow of development between Japan and the west is exactly reversed however. In Japan, technique developed over a long period of time as the result of an emerging culture of kinbaku. Culture gave birth to technique. In the west, technique has come first and has developed rapidly over a very short period of time, with a nascent culture growing up around it. Instead of the practice of kinbaku emerging from culture (as is the case in Japan) in the west we have a culture emerging from the practice of kinbaku. Technique is giving birth to culture.

Rope Culture in the West

So what does this emerging culture of kinbaku look like in the west?

First and foremost, it is technique based and is defined by people and names as much as by the actual style of rope itself. We describe ties based on who rather than what. Naka Akira's takate kote, as opposed to say, Kinoko Hajime's takate kote.

Second, how we regard those who tie in the west is also based on technique. In some cases, because they can transmit particular knowledge from Japan, often from having visited and studied there, other times because they are able to do more complicated, beautiful, extreme, or painful rope. For some, pictures on Fetlife's Kinky & Popular can lead to praise, popularity, teaching opportunities, and increasing numbers of bottoms willing to be tied by them.

Third, many tend to value rope bottoms based on their ability to handle difficult, challenging, or painful ties. There is even an emerging culture where some bottoms workout and train to be able to last longer in ties or be able to hold a more beautiful pose. Bottoms are often chosen to match technique, as opposed to adapting techniques to rope partners.

Fourth, we are a suspension culture. For most in the west, suspension is seen both as a higher level of difficulty than other forms of tying and the most visually dramatic and impressive kind of tying. For many it is also a validation of skill. It also affords the ability for those who tie to experiment with new, increasingly complicated ties. Improvements in techniques are often geared toward making suspensions safer or more comfortable to extend their duration.

Fifth, we are becoming a culture where ties are "performed" in the sense that we believe they should be done a particular way, look a particular way, and create a particular effect. When ties are taught, the "why" of the tie is usually based on effect, not affect. How a tie "feels" is usually a question of sensation, rather than emotion.

Finally, rope in the west, for a lot of people, has become a test of skill, both for tops and bottoms. The closest analogy I can think of is something like a culture of extreme sport. Innovation in kinbaku is analogous to snowboarders learning their next trick. In the same way, if your trick gets popular enough, you even get to put your name on it.

Our communities may define what we do, but it is our culture that defines why we do it.

Kinbaku: Affect and Effect

I had a moment of clarity after an afternoon spent with Naka Akira at his *kinbiken* meeting in Tokyo. For six hours, Naka sensei spoke and tied three different women. He didn't teach or even talk about a single technique. There was no instruction and no hands-on tying by any of the 30 people in attendance. What he did talk about was history, culture, and the heart of kinbaku. I couldn't help but wonder what other westerns would have thought of the day.

It is the difference between appreciation and learning. No skills were shared. There was nothing to be "learned" in the strictest sense of the word. It was, however, a masterclass in kinbaku appreciation. It was the essence of why we tie as affect, rather than effect. (I will be writing a more extensive discussion of the day in another article).

I could not have been more grateful for the day. It was the kind of learning that, for me, helps me better understand myself, my partners, and my desires. It is also the kind of learning I feel like we are missing in the west. I think that we, as a culture of rope and kinbaku, are lesser for it.

Whether a space for that kind of learning and understanding will ever emerge in the west is, I believe, an open question. Whether it will last in Japan beyond this current generation is also a great unknown.

VISITING KINBIKEN: REMEMBERING NUREKI

January 2017

On December 4th, I had the pleasure of visiting Naka Akira's second meeting of *Kinbiken*. The group takes it name from a shortened version of 緊縛美研究会, or "Kinbakubi kenkyūkai" which translates to something like "the society for the study of beautiful bondage." The meeting is a continuation of a series of gatherings started in 1986, led by Nureki Chimuo, Naka sensei's teacher and mentor.

The event would lead to a series of videos and the publication of a magazine, 緊美研通信, *Kinbiken Communication*.

Even though Nureki passed away in 2013, his presence was still felt throughout the day. In fact, I would go as far as to say the memory of Nureki was a consistent theme in almost everything Naka sensei discussed.

I have chose to call these articles "Visiting Kinbiken" because so much of what I felt was that in this space I was truly that, a visitor. Just the name itself *Kinbiken* evokes for me a history and culture that I feel I have only a limited grasp on. Even with expert translators, it was challenging to grasp the subtlety of much of what was said. As such, what I am sharing in these articles is as much an interpretation of events as it is *reportage*. In many cases, the thoughts and feelings Naka sensei expressed seemed very personal and I was left feeling that in many cases they were things best left to him to share himself.

One thing that was a core part of the experience was both Naka sensei and *Kinbiken's* connection to Nureki.

It was clear, as the day progressed, that for Naka sensei, Nureki's role in the world of kinbaku was about much more than just his tying, it was about how he chose to share that skill and how he helped define and shape the culture of kinbaku that we still participate in today.

A lot of what Naka sensei discussed were specific memories of his teacher, from his general sensibilities to specific details, right down to how Nureki would massage his new rope with his fingers, inch by inch to break it in (rope, Naka explained, was much rougher and hard to work with in those days and required a lot more preparation). He explained that rope was oiled to make it heavier so it made a strong impression when it would hit the tatami mat when you were tying.

In the audience of about 30 people, a handful had been former attendees of *Kinbiken* in the 1980s, who also shared many memories of the early days of *kinbiken* during the breaks.

What was most striking to me was Naka sensei's desire to maintain a link to the past, to the history of kinbaku and to keep alive Nureki's memory. Nureki, he told the room, was quite famous for "barking" at the rope community. He was a man of very strong opinions and was never shy about sharing them and frequently did, both at kinbiken and later through his blog. It was not clear if it was planned or inspired by the moment, but Naka announced to the room that he felt the need to begin taking on that role. And bark he did.

Between tying three different models for the day (which will be the subject of part 2), Naka sensei elaborated on many themes, but for me, three stood out as being critically important to his way of thinking about kinbaku. His opinions were delivered directly and, in some cases, harshly. The points I want to emphasize are, I believe, related and speak to a larger question, not only about how we practice kinbaku, but of what, at its core, Naka sensei believes kinbaku is about.

It was well known that Nureki had a strong dislike for rope performance and that sentiment was echoed by Naka sensei. He suggested that performance often presents kinbaku in a context that misses the essential communication between the people engaging in the act. His first tie of the afternoon was a demonstration of that feeling, pushing his model to the edge of what she could manage and repeatedly pulling back and pushing again. Finding those edges, for Naka sensei, was what he described as the essence of kinbaku and was something not possible in performance. Naka went on to say that he will be reducing the number of performances he will do over the next year.

Later in the day, Naka brought up the topic of injury and risk, being somewhat critical of recent discussions of rope injury in the community. Injuries, he explained, are a part of doing kinbaku, especially when you are playing with the edges. When working at a very high level, particularly with semenawa, it is not reasonable to expect that models will always walk away unscathed. He spoke about the various injuries he had caused over the years, including some serious ones with people he knew well and had worked with for many years.

His point was not that we shouldn't tie safely or that we shouldn't pay attention to the risks of tying, but that when you are exploring the edges and doing risky things, accidents are much more likely to happen. He described his work with Sugiura sensei as constantly pushing the envelope, always looking for the limits of kinbaku in order to capture the extremes.

The danger, Naka said, was not in the controlled environment that he ties in. Models, as well as bakushi, all know the risks and have decades of experience in creating the scenes that are captured. The risk comes when those without the training and experience see these dramatic poses and attempt to recreate them on their own.

The final concern that Naka sensei expressed was with the popularity and commercialization of kinbaku. The risk he spoke of, as I understood him, was not the accessibility or amount of kinbaku being done, but the effect that the exposure has had on the art itself. Like Nureki, Naka sensei, expressed a strong desire for kinbaku to remain *hentai*, preserving a feeling of both eroticism and perversion. It is a feeling he has expressed before in different contexts. Staying outside the mainstream is something that he expressed was very important to maintaining the integrity of the art and that integrity comes from the things he discussed throughout: pushing boundaries and creating connection and communication.

The revival of *Kinbiken* is much more than just a rope event or a venue for sharing kinbaku; it is a kind of memorial. The memory of Nureki sensei was very much alive and being channeled through Naka in his comments and his tying throughout the afternoon.

Even the choice of the name speaks to a deeper issue emerging in kinbaku. As we witness the passing of many of the first generation of rope masters, we find ourselves losing more and more touch with the history of the art. While change and growth are inevitable, forgetting our past creates the risk of losing touch with the deeper parts of what kinbaku is and can mean to those who practice it and see it as a way to share and communicate with their partners.

For Naka sensei, like Nureki before him, kinbiken is a way to share a way of thinking about kinbaku that transcends the question of *how* we tie and delves into the deeper and more complicated question of *why* we tie.

I was honored to be able to spend the day with so many others and enjoy a small taste of what that means.

LEARNING FROM THE PAST: SHOWA ERA ROPE AND THE FUTURE OF KINBAKU

January 2017

Lately I have been reviewing a lot of older style rope, primarily focused on Nureki Chimuo's instructional videos from Fuji Planning. I am really happy that I am able to make those available to people for the first time in the West on my download site at Japanese Bound.

Apart from just making a sales pitch for these videos, I want to outline a couple of reasons why I think they are important for the Western rope community, not only as an historical documentation of where many of our techniques originated, but also as a point of discussion for where rope is going, particularly in the West.

As most readers of *Kinbaku Today*, already know, Nureki Chimuo had a wide and pervasive influence of rope and rope culture in Japan. He was an author, editor, and prolific bakushi. His work with Sugiura Norio defined the aesthetics of kinbaku in Japan for decades and his influence lives on perhaps most directly in the work of Naka Akira, who is widely acknowledged as Nureki's sole deshi.

One of the most important things about Nureki's work (and I would extend this to most of those who follow in the line of Minomura Kou) to me was his focus on using rope to create an effect and a response in his partner. His goal was always to develop a tie in concert with his partner's responses to his rope. Finding the edges and limits of what his partner could endure, enjoy, and experience. That meant every part of every tie mattered.

To watch Nureki tie was always a masterclass in understanding progression, the creation and building of various forms and forces which would elicit a response and which would create a feeling of both endurance and ecstasy in his partner. Often those progressions would end in a suspension, if only as a way to maximize the tension, pressure, and intensity of the kinbaku. But suspension itself, it seems to me, never really seemed to be the point. It was only one more tool, never the end point or the goal of the tie itself.

We spend a lot of time dissecting and learning ties themselves, but very little time understanding the dynamics of scene building or rope progression.

When I see innovation in rope today, which as been happening at an incredible rate, it almost always seems geared to the question of how we make suspensions safer. The evolution and number of versions of the takate kote alone in the past five years have seemed to be focused almost exclusively on this problem and almost always targeted at the goal of making dynamic suspensions safer for the bottom.

I have no intention of suggesting this is not a praiseworthy goal or that we should stop doing that kind of work. Safety is important and performance based kinbaku has undoubtedly become the norm in the Western world of kinbaku (and arguably in Japan as well). What I do want to suggest is that we have been missing an series of opportunities to understand rope, not only historically, but as a future path of learning, development, and exploration as well.

There is an entire history of rope that has either been overlooked or discarded as uninteresting or useless because it doesn't fit into the performance model of kinbaku. These ties, some of which are suited only for floor work, static suspensions, or partial suspensions, tend not to be taught, understood or developed because they, frankly, would be dangerous in the context of dynamic suspensions or show-style kinbaku.

When we remove these from our repertoire, we need to ask ourselves what we are losing and of what we are depriving ourselves. Showa era rope has a lot to offer if we broaden our perspective to think of things like shame-based ties, predicament bondage, tying to objects (bamboo, hashira, and furniture), ties for exposure and sex. The list goes on and on.

In the rush to learn suspensions, I believe we have left many other venues unexplored. Looking back at rope from the era of Showa, there are remarkable constructions and ties that accomplish many of things beyond putting someone in the air.

It is my hope that as we look back at the history and development of kinbaku, we can think about mining the past not only as a series of techniques, but also as a philosophy and understanding of what kinbaku can be. Doing so opens up new ways of thinking and provides us with the impetus to develop and innovate in ways that can help makes us more connected to the people we tie and who tie us.

REMEMBERING YUKIMURA HARUKI (MAY 11, 1948- MARCH 3, 2016)

March 2017

I met Yukimura sensei in 2010. It was a brief meeting and I was a bit star struck. I left his apartment in Ebisu that day with a signed copy of *Transbody Bondage*, which signed with brush and ink. I hadn't learned of his passion for shodo yet, so it was a surprise to me. He also gave me a gift of photo images, stills from the movie *Bakushi*, which I framed and keep in my home dojo area. He was nice enough to let me take a few pictures with him. I didn't know it then, but that would be a turning point in my life.

Not long after, I was back in Tokyo, again sitting in his apartment in Ebisu, sipping tea and discussing arrangements for him to visit Los Angeles and teach workshops. It was the first time a Japanese rope master would come to the US to teach and it was a complicated process, more than we even knew. What only a handful of people knew at the time was that he had been diagnosed with the illness that would ultimately claim his life 5 years later.

Against what was probably good advice, he still came to LA and taught. He had given his word and he was not willing to break it, even though no one would have thought twice about it if he had.

That trip changed my life.

I had so many questions and got to spend two weeks which him, undoubtedly testing his patience and inexhaustible good will. I learned more about rope from spending time with him talking than I did in all my lessons combined. That was a pattern that would continue throughout all of our interactions over the years.

Yukimura was a genius with rope. He once told me he knew more than 100 one rope ties and I would always be amazed at his creativity with his ties. He had spent his life stripping away everything that wasn't essential to each and every tie. One rope would often be enough because every inch of it mattered, it told a story, it expressed his feeling, it brought his ties and his essence to life.

More than that, however, Yukimura was a genius with people. Students, models, fellow bakushi, friends. They all met a man who was tireless in his commitment to sharing what he loved about the world. Always with a smile, a kind word, a gesture or an exclamation of "hazukashii!" when you had gotten your tie just right and produced the effect we were always looking for.

My last visit with sensei was in December of 2015. We had many long discussions during that visit, but one in particular stuck with me. One of the things that I had wanted to talk about was devoting my dojo to a Yukimura Ryuu dojo full time. It was in many ways a scary conversation to have, but he quickly set my mind at ease. Yes it would be fine, he told me, but there was something I needed to know. Students will come to you and rope will make their relationships better, but for some it will become the thing that splits them up. You must be ready for this and you must always take care of your students.

Over my years learning from Yukimura sensei, I learned about rope, psychology, play, and emotion. But more than anything, I learned how to be a better teacher, how to share what I learned and how to do it with a spirit of love, generosity, and humor. Yukimura knew how to take care of people, whether they were models, students or fellow bakushi.

In Japanese, when you meet someone you can say "yoroshiku onegaishimasu." Like many phrases in Japanese it can be translated many ways. One of those ways is "Please take care of me."

When I think back to the time we spent together I can think of no better summary of my experience with the man I was privileged to call sensei.

In memory of his passing, words fail me. The best I can do it this:

"Thank you for taking care of me, sensei."

CONNECTION AND COMMUNICATION

March 2017

Connection and communication. These two words are often used interchangeably when it comes to discussing rope. I have always tried to use these words carefully and independently because they have very different meanings for me.

When people use the word connection in rope, what I think they are describing is a common reaction to a shared experience. She tied me the way I like to be tied. We feel the same way about the rope we do. He did this thing that I really liked. Connection is a form of recognizing a common interest in another and can often be intensified by feeling outside of the mainstream. Loving rope itself is a form of connection at least in part because it is taboo to most people in our culture.

I remember a story of two students who found themselves hiking in Nepal. They wound up in the same bar, both of them unable to speak the language, surrounded by Nepalese, barely able to order a drink. Much to their surprise, they discovered not only were they both Americans and both college students; they actually went to the same college. At that moment, you can understand why they would feel a very deep connection. They shared a huge number of things in a context where everything they experienced in their regular and daily lives was alien.

So when we talk about rope as connection, I believe that is what we mean. A connection happens based on shared experience, to greater or lesser degrees. The more you share that experience, the deeper the connection.

Interpretation of experience can converge or diverge. Connection is, in that sense, a measure of how much the interpretation of an experience converged. When they converge to a very high degree, it can feel almost magical.

Communication in rope is something I spend a lot of time thinking about, learning, and teaching. What it means to me is something different from connection (though not mutually exclusive). It asks the question, "Can I communicate what I am thinking and feeling to my partner using rope, instead of words?"

Communication with rope has two components: expression and listening.

When I start a rope scene, it may look something like this.

My partner kneels in front of me. I am behind her out of view, not yet sitting. I wait. I let her start to think about what is to come, to anticipate. I let the time pass until it starts to become awkward. I wait until something happens, a movement, a sigh, something to break the mounting tension. Now I slide my hand along her side and grab her left wrist. In that moment and with that touch, I start to tell her what I want from her. And she starts to communicate back to me. As I draw her hand behind her, I pay attention, I listen. Is she silent or making noise? Has her breathing changed? Can I feel the heat of her body as I press closer? Can she feel me?

I wait again, just one hand pinned behind her. Our communication begins. Move and countermove. Touch and response. By the time I take her right hand and bring it behind her, I know more about her, how things will be. Was she passive or resistant? What have I told her about myself?

I can tell by the way she is tilting her head that she is already starting to get lost in the feelings, but I won't let her go there. I want her present and communicating, not retreating into her own world. I press into her as I wrap the rope around her wrists, tying it and twisting to tell her she is tied and not going anywhere.

Her whimper tells me she understands.

Each wrap of the gote sends a message and begins to prepare her for what is coming. Somewhere inside, she can feel me growing more distant, leaving her alone with her feelings, encouraging to show her more of herself if she wants me back. She feels the message and begins to squirm at my touch, leaning toward me, wanting more of me.

My rope is telling her that if she wants her pleasure, she is going to have to pay for it with her shame. I want to see the vulnerable, helpless, exposed girl inside. The one she hides from the rest of the world. As I tie her ankle and raise it up, bending her knee and forcing her legs to spread wide, I am telling her she can't hide from me. I see her. Not just her nakedness, but that girl who hides that part of herself to stay safe. As my hands slide up her thighs, she knows I am here to take that safety from her.

She turns her face away, unable to look at me. I stand and move away, admiring her bound form, her spread legs, the wetness that she can't help and can't hide. I casually brush her hair off her face, not letting her hide there either.

I watch her move and twist in the rope. Her shame and embarrassment grow deeper, the longer our play continues. She tries to raise her hips to me, to offer herself to me. In that moment, the safety is gone, she has let go and shown me what she is, what she needs. She can't take it back.

I slide the rope between her legs, gently caressing her, allowing it to penetrate her lips, but barely brush her clit. She knows I want her to give in to the rope completely, to my rope, to me. I let the teasing continue until she shows me more, abandoning any sense of a calm or security. Finally, she begins to cry as I press the rope against her clit and hold it there as she grinds against it, exploding in orgasm after orgasm.

What is important to me about that kind of rope is that it could have gone a thousand different ways. The power of that kind of scene, which is the kind of rope i enjoy, is that we are both present with each other, sharing, communicating and responding to one another.

I often read posts from bottoms about how they feel in rope. But rarely, if ever, do they talk about what they give to their partners. I often read post from tops about how they tie. But rarely, if ever, do they talk about how they share their feelings, thoughts, and intentions through their rope.

My partner doesn't drift off to her own world, because she is trying to communicate with me. She can't do that if she is lost in her own world. She has to be in mine or ours, more to the point. Likewise, I can't just let my intention be the whole scene, I need to adjust and finesse that. If I want her to give part of herself to me, I have to tell her what I want. I have to be able to use my rope to do that.

Therein lies the greatest difference between connection and communication. Connection only requires a mutually shared and understood experience. Communication requires an active and ongoing transmission of feeling, emotion, and intention that is built by listening and responding to each other.

Because connection is based in experience, tops and bottoms can retreat into their inner worlds, bliss out, enjoy the aesthetics and have a deeply connected experience. Like finding yourself in a bar in Nepal, you don't need to communicate; you only need to share the experience.

Communication is building that experience as a give and take or expression and listening. Instead of retreating to your inner world, you actively and intentionally share it. That is true for both the top and the bottom.

When I tie, I want to tie the person, not their body. I can only work with what they give me. By the same token, they can only trust me with the deepest part of themselves if they know I am offering the same in return.

Connection comforts us, because in it we find a mirror to our interpretation of the world. Communication exposes us. It makes us raw and vulnerable, so when we do connect it is to something deep that we have built together.

Even in something like semenawa, we can see an evolution of connection through communication. A rope scene that starts with "I want to hurt you" and "I want to hurt" can be deeply connected with almost no communication at all. But once it becomes about suffering, it requires more communication. Ultimately, a semenawa scene where you know not just how your partner is suffering for you but why, can only be accomplished with communication. You know it because you are listening to her and she knows why she is suffering because you have told her with your rope. In that moment you have not just shared an experience, you have shared the deepest part of yourselves.

THE FLOW OF INK
AND ROPE

March 2017

One of the hardest things about learning Japanese calligraphy (shodō) for me has always been the fact that you are forbidden to go back and correct any mistakes you make. If a line is too short or it is finished improperly, you don't go back and fix it.

There is a feeling you get when you start writing with the brush that is unlike anything else. When the ink meets the paper, it is a moment of permanence. It is a commitment. Each stroke that follows is the same way. As much as it makes the task more difficult, it is also what gives it meaning.

From time to time, the temptation to go back and just add a little more ink can be overwhelming. But if you do, your teacher can always tell. So can anyone looking at it. Something just feels off about corrected shodō.

This weekend, I was quite surprised when Murasaki sensei made the same analogy with rope. Tying is like shodō, she said. When you tie the gote you let the ropes stay where you put them. You shouldn't go back and change them. They represent a commitment, which is worth getting right the first time.

Iroha san, likewise, explained that it always breaks her concentration when someone tying her stops the flow of the tie and goes back to adjust the ropes.

It feels to me that treating shibari the way we treat shodō gives us yet another way to honor the moment, the presence of our partner, and making a commitment to our time together.

Quelle Surprise or "I Tie and I Know Things"
August 2017

The events of the past year or two in the rope community haven't come as much of a surprise to me. I haven't been part of that community for a long time and the reason why has a lot to do, I believe, with what has been happening.

For the past decade, I have been warning people of the problems and limitations of focusing kinbaku so intensely on technique, without thinking about the heart of it. The focus has been, almost exclusively, on the how to tie, rather than the why we tie. And by why, I don't mean "why we use a munter hutch here, rather than there." I mean motivation. I mean passion. I mean desire. I mean fantasy. **I mean heart**.

For me, it has always been simple. I want to tie someone so I can see a part of them they can only reveal when in rope. I want to evoke and provoke feelings of embarrassment, shame, and arousal. I want to share the part of myself that desires to see that with the part of them that wants to show it and give it to me.

None of that has anything to do with technique or even rope really. Those are my motivations. No one else needs to share them, other than the person I am tying with.

If you get tied by me in a rope scene (which for me requires some form of relationship, usually over a long period of time) that is what you are going to get and you will have no ambiguity about it.

The issue I have with rope education as I have seen it practiced is that the focus on technique has produced an unintended consequence and a rather serious one.

We all know the maxim that knowledge is power. In the rope

world it has also taken on an added element. Rope is entitlement.

If you learn enough technique, you begin to feel you are entitled. You are entitled to the best play spaces. To the prettiest girls or boys. To getting what you want from a scene. To taking what you want from your partners.

You invested your time. You practiced. You learned the technique. Now you get the payoff.

Technique becomes about ego and it becomes about validation. You tie to show others how much you know and what you can do. Your partners become props. Beautiful props, suffering in your rope.

Your technique gets validated in stage two. You become a teacher. Maybe you even have travelled to meet people and learn from them. You got their technique and now you can show it to others.

Now your entitlement extends to the whole community. You get accolades and attention because you can show people how to tie 87 hishi patterns in 30 minutes or you can explain twenty different frictions by five Japanese bakushi.

You may even have the latest news about how kannukis now are tied in an order different than they used to be.

And as we see over and over again, all that means exactly shit if your heart isn't right.

The truth is, in the rope community no one talks about or values heart. They give it lip service all the time. Everyone is into "connective rope" and the way they go about it is to teach a class on "connective rope techniques," almost, but not entirely, completely missing the point.

You value technique. You may as well order GOT T-shirts saying "I Tie and I Know Things" because that seems to be the value system of the rope community today.

So, it comes as no surprise to me that some of the top "riggers" in the rope community end up where they do. They start to believe their reviews and they start to act on that entitlement.

But some of the blame rests with a community so hungry for learning the next pattern or the new craziest tie that they not only look past the system of entitlement they are creating–they feed it and they are complicit in it.

You make these people your idols and that is a difficult thing to resist.

You have created a world where learning the next big thing often means tolerating egos, narcissism, and people who push boundaries, often times uncomfortably. But you put up with it because these people tie and **they know things.**

And when the inevitable happens people are shocked. They are wounded and hurt. And then slowly we hear all the stories. It has been happening for years. The stories start to all sound the same.

But mostly people are pissed. Their source of knowledge has been cut off and now they feel all the poorer for it. I think that is where a lot of the anger and disappointment comes from, to be honest.

What people fail to see is that everything you were learning was tainted from the beginning.

On a personal note, I can say in six years in studying with my teacher in Tokyo, I never once asked him how to do something.

Technique was always second to heart. One of my most precious memories of him was when he told me, "I can tell you understand me, because of the questions you ask." They were always questions about heart. Many of those conversations made me the person I am today, not just in rope, but in life.

I am not trying to tell anyone how to do what they do. I am just saying a lot of people need to look in the mirror and take responsibility for the world they created and the consequences of it.

I am absolutely certain that I will change nothing by writing this, but at least now people can't say "No one ever told me."

ROPE AND TRUST

March 2018

It seems like every time I go to Tokyo a theme emerges from the trip. This time the theme is trust.

With any kind of business dealings in Japan, trust or shinrai (信頼) is the foundation of most relationships. Making the effort to travel to Japan and sit across from people and be able to look them in the eye when you discuss things is important and it makes a huge difference in the kinds of things you can get accomplished.

When I talked with my business partner in Japan about visiting, they suggested it would be helpful, so most of the week I had meetings with people who I have been building that trust relationship with for the past year. Sitting with them they opened up in ways they never would have communicating at a distance.

It got me thinking about how the Japanese approach tying as well. In Japan, the concept of consent is not something that is embraced or even particularly well understood. I think the deeper notion of shinrai takes the place of consent and creates a different feeling of security and safety.

During a meeting with Randa Mai, I asked him why he started performing and his answer was straightforward: he wanted to show audiences that kinbaku is fundamentally about trust. He wanted people to see the level of trust that not only could exist, but *must* exist for two people to play together in an SM show.

Rope and SM, he explained, was about shinrai.

As I began to think more about this, I started to ask around. My friend Desi La told me I needed to look at the concept of makaseru, which means to entrust something to someone else. A concept he felt was a deep part of Japanese culture.

If you have ever been to a sushi bar where the chef chooses your meal, you may be familiar with the concept of omakase, which roughly translates to "I'll leave it up to you." The word omakase comes from makaseru and embodies that notion of trusting your well-being to another.

More and more, I was finding the idea of shinrai and makaseru appearing in Japanese culture. In particular, it seems to be a foundation for how Japanese tend to think about rope relationships as well.

Unlike the western notion of consent, which presupposed that you know what is going to happen when you tie (e.g. you can only consent to something you have knowledge of), trust presupposes exactly the opposite. Trust is based on the unknown. We don't trust a sushi chef to bring us what we consent to. We trust him to choose for us specifically *without our knowing* and based on what he or she thinks is best for us.

Trust, unlike consent, is also relational. It is built over time. It has degrees and granularity. It evolves. It is fragile and requires nurturing and patience. All things that the Western mind has trouble with. Trust relationships are never black and white.

On the other hand, consent is binary. Either you have it or you don't. It can be given or withdrawn with a word at any time for any reason or for no reason at all. It is fast, clear, easy, and direct. It removes the nebulous human element (or at least purports to) and replaces it with logical, legalistic simplicity.

I think the western need for consent and our constant discussion of it is born from a more fundamental issue: *We don't trust each other very much.*

One of the beautiful things about tying in Japan, at least in my experience, is that the relationship, from the first time you tie together, begins with trust. I feel that when I tie here. My partner has entrusted their well-being to me. It feels sacred and fragile. I know out relationship will be different after the tie than when it started, hopefully for the better.

I feel it too at home, but only because I have relationships that took years to build that kind of connection. It was an effect of prolonged experience, not an assumption that those relationships were built on.

I have begun to wonder if consent is a clumsy solution to a much bigger problem. Maybe what we need to think about in the west is building a culture of trust. A consent mindset presumes a lack of trust at the outset, so much so that in order to specify that we trust someone, we are forced to use the Orwellian sounding construct of "consensual non-consent." When we say that, what we really mean is trust.

Just as it is not part of our culture to sit down at a restaurant and say "Surprise ne,' it is also not part of our culture to value trust in our relationships, even our D/s ones. It is certainly not our starting place.

The problem may be intractable. I don't know. Maybe embracing consent in the west is just as necessary as embracing shinrai in Japan. I see people working so hard to make consent culture work here. Every time I see a campaign like "Consent is sexy" or "Consent rocks" I cringe a little bit. We generally don't need to be told what is and isn't sexy or what does and doesn't rock. We've never needed a campaign like "sex is fun!" because, for the most part, no one needs to be convinced.

I think we need to be more concerned about why we, as a culture, need this legalistic prophylactic before we can even touch each other.

What brought things full circle to me was tying with a woman named Mari at bakuyukai on Saturday night. I asked her what style of tying she most preferred.

Her answer: "Omakase."

THE RUSH TO SUSPEND

September 2018

People are often quick to write about how suspension is not the end all and be all of rope bondage and how floor work is better and how simple ties can be even better, etc. etc. etc.

It is a philosophy I happen to agree with. But it would be disingenuous to suggest that that is the first place people exploring rope will end up.

I remember when I first learned suspensions.

I really loved doing them because I felt they were a true test of skill. I still believe that, even though I rarely do them anymore.

I probably had more than 100 hours of one on one instruction before I did my first suspension. Before I did my first one I was given a simple challenge. I had to tie a 3 rope takate kote three times with the same tension (based on feeling the tension and feedback from the bottom).

It is a good exercise. If you haven't tried it, I encourage you to tie your partner three times in a row with what you feel is exactly the same tension and placement. If you can't do this consistently, I would suggest spending more time working on your tension before suspending someone.

But that isn't what I wanted to write about.

What has surprised me more than anything else is the number of times I see descriptions and scenes or photos of suspensions with the caption "first time in rope" or words to that effect.

When I was doing suspensions, I had a rule. I wouldn't suspend someone until I had tied them at least three times. If you can't come up with at least three smoking hot scenes not involving a suspension, your suspensions are probably not going to be all that interesting.

One of the most moving scenes I have ever witnessed was Naka Akira tying Iroha. There was no hard point, bamboo, or shiten. All floor work. It was so moving, many people were moved to tears. In my case, I just had something in my eye.

The reason for tying multiple times pre-suspension was simple. I needed to learn how they responded to my rope. Tying for play and working with them allows you to learn whatever their small quirks are as well as how they react to your rope. You learn what their reactions mean, how to read them, and how to tie them effectively. Your learn the best placement and what tensions work for them.

At the time I was doing suspensions there were not very many experienced rope bottoms and very few discussions of rope bottoming. Today, there are many, many more bottoms who have outstanding body awareness, communication skills, and the ability to help navigate tricky situations.

But there are far more new bottoms. Many of whom do not know how to communicate in rope or what ties work best for them.

Maybe I am just old. Or old fashioned. But I don't really understand the rush to suspend someone, especially their first time in rope. Take the time to learn about them and for them to learn about themselves.

When we tie, and especially when we do suspensions, we rely a lot on our partners to communicate with us about what is going on. When you are brand new to rope you have neither the vocabulary nor the experience to give feedback.

So what is the rush to get people up in the air?

ROPE IS EASY; FEELING NOT SO MUCH

November 2018

I have been teaching rope for a while. Actually, that isn't true. I have been teaching people how to communicate with each other using rope for a while.

There is a difference between the two.

Years ago, I asked Chiba Eizo what the difference was between shibari in the west in in Japan. And he said (paraphrasing). In Japan, we start with heart (心) and then teach technique (形). In the west, it seems that everyone starts with technique and we hope they find the heart.

I just read a post about that discussed learning rope like we learn driving.

It feels like that is mostly what we do in the west.

I once asked someone what "labbing" was, which was a term I had never heard before. Once they explained it to me, I asked if people ever "labbed" communication or how they expressed feeling and emotion in rope. They told me they had never heard of anyone doing that and when I asked "Why not?" they said it was too hard and too complicated.

More or less, that is what I find lacking these days.

Feeling, emotion, depth. Conveying those things in rope is hard. It can take a lifetime to learn. And, as sorry as I am to say it, those things have nothing to do with technique.

You may be able to tie a Naka Akira version of the most elaborate suspension you can imagine, but without the feeling, you are missing something very, very fundamental.

What do I mean by feeling? That is the heart, the kororo, the essence of why one ties.

I can't quite explain it. And this is a huge part of the problem. It is really fucking hard to explain and doubly hard to teach.

So we don't.

With my more advanced students, I do an exercise where during a tie I stop them and ask the person tying "What is she feeling right now?" and then "What do you want her to be feeling?"

More often than not, the responses is "I don't know."

Because we don't teach it. We don't think about it and it isn't part of the emotional fabric of western shibari. Without that, we are going through the motions. We are treating our shibari like it is driving instruction.

And maybe that is OK for most people. For me, I would prefer not to treat my partner like they were car.

I once was fortunate enough to watch Nureki Chimuo tie. By the end of the second rope of his takate kote, his model had orgasmed twice. Countless times I watched Yukimura sensei drop women into subspace with a one rope gote. That was never about technique.

I can teach you Yukimura's gote in an hour. Learning how to use it to communicate feelings, emotions, and heart? That can take a lifetime.

If we reduce rope to learning how to drive a car, all it will ever be is learning how to drive a car.

There is so much more. If all you ever do is learn how to tie, you will never learn why you tie. And without that, you will end up missing the best parts

MY BEST ROPE TEACHERS HAVE ALL BEEN BOTTOMS

April 2019

I have been lucky to have been taught by some of the top rope masters in the world, and particularly fortunate to have studied closely with one of Japan's grand masters.

They taught me a lot about rope and how to tie.

But the most valuable insights and what changed the most about how I tie has been the lessons I have learned from the people I have tied.

Patterns, knots, ties, poses, and positions are relatively easy. Communication is more challenging. The only person who can tell you what you communicate with your rope is the person inside it.

One bottom in particular, the recent subject of a post about tsuyoi (strength in bottoming), has been formative in my understanding of rope. She often served as my bottom for lessons in Japan and at the end of each session she would give honest and very useful feedback on how I did. Each time it was like a series of epiphanies. I learned from her what I was communicating. The good and the bad. I learned how to do it better. I learned what I wanted for myself and what I wanted from my partners.

She taught me how to listen and how to share my feelings through rope. Those who I tie now, all do the same. It is the one thing I look for in rope partners.

Learning to tie, for me at least, is a process of listening to your partner. Before, during, and after. Every action and every inter-action is an opportunity to learn about them and to learn about yourself.

When people ask me why I tie, that is my answer. To learn about my partner and to learn about myself.

In that journey, it has been my partners who have taught me more in both regards, than any teacher, instructor, book or video.

I hope in some small way, I have been able to share myself with them and provide them the same opportunity.

The "Elitism" of Japanese Rope

May 2019

I started tying in 2006 or 2007. I can't really remember, exactly. But what I do remember was that when I started tying in America, almost no one was doing shibari. The few people that were had pieced together techniques by reverse engineering images or working from a handful of how-to materials that were hard to find and in a language they didn't understand.

That started to change around 2011. Japan started to open up, with bakushi coming to visit the US at first, followed by more and more westerners going to Japan. That evolution happened earlier in Europe, I believe. But with pretty much the same effect. Technique got better at an almost exponential rate. People were learning Japanese rope techniques from Japanese masters who had spent a good portion of their lives perfecting them.

Essentially, we got a content dump with neither the time or the context to make much sense of it.

But something else happened. It opened a divide, between those who were getting instruction first hand and those who weren't. Anyone who had first hand access to that knowledge started to be branded an "elitist." We we told that we were telling other people they were doing things wrong. We were all convinced we were better than those who knew less, etc. etc. etc.

The only problem with this narrative was, as far as I can tell, no one was actually saying that. In fact, those who had developed their knowledge and understanding of kinbaku were coming back, sometimes in droves, wanting to teach and share what they had learned.

I can't speak for anyone else, but my experiences learning rope in Japan got me in touch with a very personal, deeply emotional side of rope that I was as missing in most Western rope classes. That is what I wanted to share and teach. It was what my teacher and Japan was extremely good at and it is what, for me, profoundly change the way I think about rope, communication, my partner and how I tie.

Is it "better" in some sense? Well, for me it certainly was. It was better than what I knew before I studied it. Is it better for everyone? Of course not.

Yukimura would often say "rope is free," meaning people are free to do rope however they wish. It would be very un-Japanese to tell someone else what to do with their rope or how to tie, unless, of course, they come to you looking for instruction.

But here is where we face a problem.

Over the past 10 years, as we experienced a massive content and technique dump, people are not understanding where the things they are doing came from and that is a significant problem. A tie that has emerged over 20 or 30 years of trial and error, as part of a larger system, philosophy, or school of kinbaku has evolved to meet certain needs, to perform certain functions, and has to be understood within a context.

Now, either you believe that or you don't. If you don't, there is probably nothing I can say to convince you otherwise. But I am relatively certain, after talking with many of the people who tie in Japan, that the people who invented these ties believed that.

Most of the charges of "elitism" in rope, in my experience, appear to come from a place of deep insecurity. People seem terrified of being told they are wrong or that they can't do anything they like with their rope. But that is a fear they are projecting onto others. No one cares what you do with your rope. Really. No one cares.

The desire to hang on to some narrative of elitism and persecution, however, carries with it a deeper consequence.

Those who seem most invested in rope elitism, also seem the most insistent on demanding that rope is something simple, that anyone can do, and that has nothing to more complicated that tying a few knots.

It is hard for me to see these cries of elitism as coming from any place other than a deeply felt sense of insecurity. The only way to defend it is to diminish the activity itself. The only way to diminish expertise is to believe that rope itself has no depth, culture, history or meaning beyond your own naive, shallow, and solipsistic self-expression.

Herein lies the danger. You need not be around the rope world for too long before you stumble onto a debate about whether or not the takate kote is a safe tie. Nor do you have to wait long, if you live in even a small city, for someone to offer a class on how to tie it.

The takate kote is probably the most frequently taught and most frequently tied Japanese tie, both in the West and in Japan. That alone accounts for a higher rate of incidents. But so does the attitude with which it is frequently taught. The only way to teach it as widely and as frequently as we do is diminish the level of expertise required to tie and (perhaps more importantly) teach it. That is the danger of buying into the dismissal of education, research, hard work, and experience as "elitism." People get hurt.

Is the takate kote dangerous? Yes. You bet your ass it is. Which is why you need to spend a fuck ton of time and energy learning about it before you tie it. Not because it is a challenging feat of rope engineering (which it definitely can be) but because, in each school of rope, it has a long, complicated, and important evolution. And understanding that evolution is essential to understanding what that tie can and cannot do.

I learned Naka Akira's two rope gote in Japan from him personally. Maybe 2011 or 2012. We were at UBU and he gave me a lesson while we were watching one of his videos together. I also hosted him in Los Angeles in the Summer of 2014. I spent time with him and got several lessons from him in my living room, in addition to attending the workshops while he was here.

I have attended his kinbiken events, done photo shoots of his rope, and I visit with him every time I am in Japan.

Would I teach his gote? No.

Why not?

He has never asked me to. If he wanted me to teach his rope style (and if he felt I knew it well enough, which I don't), he would ask me to teach it. That is what happened to me with Yukimura sensei in 2011. He asked me to teach.

Recently, Riccadro Wildties, Naka Akira's deshi, posted something which speaks to the issue directly:

> *"Can I teach your style (after a few classes)?*
>
> *Can I be your assistant for a month?*
>
> *Can I perform in xxx (super exclusive gig in Japan)."*
>
> *When will people in the West understand they should not ask these things to Japanese masters? You put them in an uncomfortable position. It's hard for them, out of cultural politeness, to say no and to explain you why. Questions like these*

are one of the reasons Japanese masters feel uncomfortable with western students. If they want to invite you, to a show or as assistance, or want you to teach their style, they will ask you themselves. Stop making a fool out of yourself and making them feel uncomfortable! Be respectful of their work and culture!

I have little doubt that if I approached Naka sensei and asked to teach his gote, he would say yes. I am also equally certain it would make him very uncomfortable. If you have to ask, you probably shouldn't be teaching it.

Does that mean I shouldn't tie it? No, but that is a whole different question. Because teaching and tying are completely different things. When you teach you take up the mantle of the history of the tie you are teaching. When you tie it, you are doing the tie in the manner in which it was shared with you, for you, and in order to suit you. Most of the people who teach rope that I meet fail to understand the difference.

The fact that someone learned a tie from Naka sensei, or Kanna sensei, or Kazami sensei, means something. It doesn't mean they are qualified to teach it. It means they are qualified to do it (or at least have been properly instructed how to do it).

I know only a handful of people who have been asked to teach a particular style of Japanese rope by Japanese masters. I see a lot more who have "gotten permission" and then I see a ton of people who just don't give a shit and will name drop a Japanese master's name and purport to being doing their rope because that is how they learned it and they simply don't know any different.

So, the crux of the matter is this. When people dismiss those who have taken the time to study and learn and truly dedicate themselves to learning more than just the technique as "elitist" what they are doing is also dismissing the context that is required to make much of what we do safe and meaningful. They are dismissing the possibility of what rope can be, in order to hang on to and main control over what it is they already have.

As I said that the beginning, "Rope is free." What we are not free to do is have it both ways. You can't trade on the name of those who you claim to respect, while at the same time dismissing those who actually do the work to foster a deep understanding of that same style of rope as "elitists."

I recently saw a class described as a "TK that was learned in New York (teacher unspecified) which was a variation of an OS3 TK which was based on Akechi Denki's style of tying." I would have been fine with that description if it had ended with "New York." If that is elitist, so be it. But it is an elitism that is born out of a respect for what we do, the people who do it, the safety of our partners, and for the generations of bakushi who have come before us.

Tie how you like. Teach what you like. But stop credentialing yourself with the names of people who have neither given you the permission nor the qualifications to teach what they do.

Printed in the USA
CPSIA information can be obtained
at www.ICGtesting.com
LVHW092119051223
765782LV00018B/85

9 781099 161933